KBI: The Strategic Metric Advantage

KBI

THE STRATEGIC METRIC ADVANTAGE

Learn what Key Behaviour Indicators
are, their benefits over KPIs, and how
they will build the company culture and
brand you have been striving for.

RICHARD A. PERRY

First Edition 2023

Edited by Elena Muratova

ISBN: 978-0-6459630-0-7 (pbk) eISBN: 978-0-6459630-1-4 (ebook)

NATIONAL LIBRARY OF AUSTRALIA

A catalogue record for this book is available from the National Library of Australia

Dedication

There are people in my life who have given me the inspiration to stretch myself and attempt things I would never have dreamed of.

My amazing wife, Pree Perry, whose love, humanity, and positive spirit have fuelled me to try and be the best version of myself that I can be. Thank you for always having my back, asking me what I was thinking, and unquestionably supporting me on whatever pathway I wander down next.

My sons, Tom Perry & Joe Perry, who have grown into the two most wonderful human beings and given me every reason to invest in the future.

My lifelong friends:

John C. Pavey, a true legend, and the kindest, smartest, most honest person I have ever met. A never-ending source of inspiration with a uniquely quirky blend of creative and abstract thinking.

Stuart Blackery, a walking tour-de-force of curiosity, determination, and confidence that has always inspired me to keep going and find the answer.

Ryan Liddle, aka "Mr. Think Differently." Just when I think I have a grip on things, Ryan has the knack to open yet another door I didn't even know was there. I have never learned so much from just one person.

There are also people who took a chance on me, gave me that break in one of those sliding-door moments, and helped me make a huge bounce forward. I will forever be in debt to them.

Thank you, one and all.

Ian Naylor, Philip Robbins-Jones, Janine Keefe, Grant O'Brien.

Contents

Preface - Why KBIs?

This book is built upon the following fundamental logic:

- You get what you measure.
- Behaviour is Culture.
- Measure Behaviour to achieve Culture.

Key Behaviour Indicators (KBIs) offer insights into the mindset of your organisation. While this insight might come naturally to a few leaders, it remains elusive for the rest of us. This book thoroughly explores the concept of KBIs and provides a framework with step-by-step activities to bring them to life. By following this playbook, your organisation will develop the ability to genuinely understand your people and their mindsets with newfound clarity and insight.

KBIs are not mere Key Performance Indicators (KPIs) that measure individuals. KBIs aid in selecting, measuring, and optimising the behaviours that uphold your organisation's values, brand, strategy, and purpose. They play a pivotal role in constructing your organisational culture.

KPI — WHAT HAPPENED

KBI — WHAT WILL HAPPEN

- KPIs tell you what happened.
- KBIs tell you what will happen.

Behaviours are deeply ingrained and resistant to change, no matter what forces are brought to bear on an individual. We are, after all, creatures of habit. We may support change when it affects others, but we are often entrenched in our own ways and will diligently work to remain as we are. As our behaviours are exceptionally enduring and steadfast, they can therefore assist us in predicting the future.

You might ask, "Don't some KPIs, such as 'lead indicators,' predict the future too?" Even these lead indicators remain historical; they merely happen to be upstream. Their outcome simply has a direct impact on a downstream activity. They don't reveal how your team will respond to what's about to occur. You don't know how they might overcome an issue or capitalise on an opportunity. KBIs, on the other hand, do.

Think of Key Performance Indicators (KPIs) as constraints instead. More often than not, they burden your organisation. They not only consume resources to produce, explain, and investigate their existence, but they also stifle innovation and creativity by offering a narrow window of performance to aim at. KBIs offer a means to shed many of these KPIs while yielding better outcomes. A single KBI can replace hundreds of KPIs; it can also eliminate policies, procedures, business rules, and any other obstacles that hinder your workforce. This might sound chaotic, but in reality, it's quite the opposite. Most documentation caters to common situations, and hence, they're rarely used since they are at the forefront of most people's minds. When uncommon events occur, there's often no documentation or guidance for people to refer to at the very moment they really need it. KBIs, however, will guide actions that lead to outcomes aligned with the organisation's values, even without a single word having been documented.

KBIs wield exceptional power, but they do have a weak spot. They depend on the actions of leaders. If leaders don't authentically exhibit the behaviours and champion the KBIs, they will gradually recede into the background and eventually fade away. As a leader, and especially for this initiative, your primary role should be to lead by example. The handful of KBIs (around 10) that will be established will necessitate a conscious and deliberate effort initially. However, over time, like all habits, they will become second nature. Your team will follow your lead. KBIs evolve into a blueprint design for your organisation's mindset, and that mindset is what shapes your culture.

KBIs are highly cost-effective and don't need specialist IT software, complex transformation programs, or teams of consultants or psychologists. The only requirement for KBIs is to maintain personal discipline in keeping them at the forefront of your mind and demonstrating them day after day — a price easily worth paying.

Initially, KBIs might feel awkward. Organisations and their employees are accustomed to managing and enhancing elements such as processes, routines, structures, accountabilities, and more. Behaviours lack process maps, organisation charts, or set procedures to follow. To alleviate this awkwardness, we'll employ the concept of KBIs. They offer a method to make your chosen subset of behaviours tangible and to introduce some structure. This structure and mechanics for KBIs becomes a way to make the management and enhancement of behaviours both tangible and valuable.

The concept of KBIs opens a portal to untapped potential and capacity within your organisation that was previously beyond reach.

Allow me to ask you, "Who was the best manager you've ever worked for?" I presume you have that individual in mind. Now, what makes them exceptional to you? Was it their technical prowess? Their skills? Their experience? I suspect not. I propose it's due to their behaviour and how they treated you. You would readily go the extra mile for such a leader. By utilising KBIs, we can establish clearer expectations for everyone from a fresh entry-level recruit to the CEO. By selecting the appropriate KBIs (and practicing them daily), we can inspire our teams to achieve greater outcomes and derive more satisfaction in return. We will encourage our leaders to become better leaders, sparking a virtuous cycle where improved leaders grow to become exceptional leaders. Exceptional leadership is, of course, critical to unlocking latent potential and capacity within your organisation. What if everyone went the extra mile?

KBIs make the difference.

With most other factors remaining relatively equal, KBIs will unlock the full potential of your workforce; they will bridge the alignment gap necessary to attain strategic objectives and the organisation's purpose. KBIs stand as your strategic advantage.

This book provides explanations, tools, and methods necessary to enable you to introduce KBIs into your organisation. It also incorporates examples of other organisations that have (and a few that have not) followed this approach, and what happened as a result.

What's in the Book

These are the sections that will take you on a journey where you will gain a thorough understanding of what KBIs are, how you and your organisation can select and implement them, and how you can secure the long-term strategic advantage that they can provide.

1. Introduction.

This section holds the backstory of how this book came into being. This book is the result of decades of experience working with thousands of people, hundreds of leaders, and tens of organisations. It is also, to some extent, an accident. There is definitely some serendipity involved in the combination of the people I have met over the years, their roles, the organisations we have worked in and alongside, and the unique experiences that happened to us along the way.

2. What are KBIs.

In this section, you will go through an overview of the KBI concept and how they fit into the wider picture with the other tools that you have. You will also understand why KBIs are important and some of the less obvious benefits they provide, as well as the obvious big-ticket item - Culture.

3. Change Management.

You will learn some of the tactics that can be used to ease the concept of KBIs into the organisation. It is easier than most people think, but there is one key moment that will make or break how successful this initiative is.

4. The limits of KPIs.

You will examine the uses and limitations of traditional KPIs. We shall see where they are still important in operational and management contexts, but why you should remove some of them.

5. Understanding Behaviour.

You get to grips in detail with what a Behaviour is and, more importantly, what it is not. This subject is not the easiest, and it will take some practice to hone the skill of linking the outcome you want to the behaviours that contribute towards it. We will reference several models from great thought leaders in organisational and personal improvement to help shape this understanding.

6. The benefits of using KBIs.

You will focus on the expected benefits of adopting KBIs for a range of stakeholder groups and desired organisation outcomes. For example, you will examine how behaviours can improve processes, overcome issues, and deliver a better product in the operational context where a service or product is delivered to a customer. You will also explore how you can improve customer intimacy and achieve genuine customer loyalty and satisfaction. Lastly, but most importantly, you will delve into how you can improve the employee experience. This is the foundation for all other areas of improvement. We will spend a lot of time at this grassroots level as it will be the base upon which all the other achievements will be built.

7. Selecting your KBIs.

This is a practical section that will guide you in selecting the optimal set of behaviours that will suit your organisation. Believe it or not, there is no definitive list of human behaviours since it is a complex and multifaceted topic that can be influenced by various factors such as personality, social norms, environmental factors, law, regulation, and even taboo areas. However, we will step through a process to get you a set of behaviours that will shift the needle in the context of your organisation.

8. Using KBIs to bring your Culture to life.

In this section, you will pressure test your organisation's purpose, objectives, goals, and values, and then review them against your set of primary behaviours. You will probably make some adjustments to them to align and tie all these strategic elements together. This is a significant step in refreshing your company culture and refining your brand into the future. Be bold in this step. It is not uncommon to discover that by focusing on behaviours we can cause feedback and potentially require an adjustment to the company's purpose, objectives, and values. This adjustment is not only acceptable but is also essential; sometimes, it takes a new perspective like this one to finally polish the words that have been your 'north star' so far. This section will walk you through a roadmap on how to gain support for the notion of KBIs and how to bring about the implementation of KBIs into your organisation.

9. Case studies.

You will review several case studies where a deliberate focus on behaviours and culture has (and has not) happened in other organisations. This section will also address the sensitive fact that today, it is becoming increasingly delicate to comment constructively about someone without the possibility of offending them. You will look at how we can professionally and fairly measure behaviours so that they are mutually trusted.

10. A double-click on Trust.

In this section, you will take a slight detour to focus on behaviours that lead to trust and why this area is so important in the realm of KBIs.

11. Notes for CEOs.

This section provides specific guidance for the leader of the organisation to help introduce, implement, and embed KBIs. You will also find some specific support in leading this change with authenticity and conviction.

Conclusion

As you would expect, this is a summary and recap of what you have been through and brings you back full circle.

Hopefully, after reading the contents of this book, you will be clear on the benefits of KBIs, and you will have the knowledge to implement them with confidence.

Acknowledgements

Many other sources of research, documentation, publication, and examples were reviewed in the writing of this book. I have listed them in this section and fully recognise their standalone contributions and thank them all for their work.

SECTION 1
Introduction

....

In a way, the purpose and intent of this book is to save you from the same fate as myself. You see, there is a trap that we all fall into: we get stuck on "doing" and forget about "learning". This book shares my single most important learning from over 40 years of professional corporate life - a meandering thread of knowledge that will give you the inside line on securing a strategic advantage for your organisation. It has such a significant impact that it is the one (and only) thing I want to pass on.

I have some assumptions. I assume that you would agree that having an aligned, engaged, and invested team that is obsessed with customer loyalty, doing the right thing, and striving for success is seen as a positive thing. Also, I assume that you believe that having effortless, unrelenting, and sustainable improvement capability throughout your organisation is also highly desirable and valuable. Would it also be true that you would rather not spend millions on consultants, new systems, education programs, or large-scale transformation initiatives to achieve it? Are we on the same page?

There is a mountain of latent capability and capacity in your organisation right now. The KBI concept in this book will help you find it, inspire it, harness it, and bring it to life for yourself, your team, and your organisation.

Industrial Engineers develop an interesting skill as they critically study people at work. They look at the obvious elements like 'what people do', and detailed elements like 'how they do it' and even 'why they do it'. As such, there is a lot of data captured during these work studies, so this data is categorised in certain ways to make it easier to work with. One of these ways is quite useful for us. It is a categorisation of

> Somebody could spend all day doing something, but what was it they should have actually been doing.

whether the work 'needed' to be done or not. Somebody could spend all day doing something, but what was it they should have actually been doing. The three buckets that are most commonly used to categorise this are Must-do, Should-do, and Could-do. Must-do is critical. If this does not get done, then the desired outcome is never achieved. Should-do creates a better outcome, one that is valued by someone, but is not critical to the outcome. Could-do is anything else that may or may not add any immediate value.

Let's assume that the Must-do work in your organisation is consistently done, maybe sometimes with little intervention, maybe sometimes with a lot. Now, how much Should-do gets done? During most of the work studies I have seen and been a part of, less than half of the Should-do work ever gets done. People find workarounds, cut corners, avoid it altogether and hope they don't get caught. All this avoidance (which usually actually takes up time and cunning thinking) means someone else is probably negatively impacted, or the outcome 'just about' meets the minimum standard, when perhaps a higher benchmark is within reach.

Instead of the organisation being content with doing the minimum Must-do activities, KBIs and the impact they bring will shift the needle and give everyone throughout the organisation the internal personal reasons they need to do everything they Should-do and maybe even Could-do to achieve better and better results.

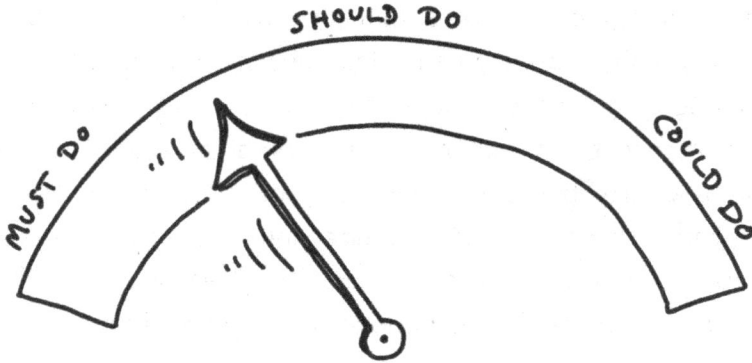

SHOULD DO

MUST DO

COULD DO

How have I learned this? I am not from an academic profession or formally educated about the inner workings of the brain, psychology, or neuroscience. Yes, I have read a little about them, and maybe it is fair to say that I have a grip on some of the fundamentals, but that is all. I have, however, been involved in problem-solving, change, business improvement, productivity, and transformation programs for all of my working life. In theory, if I were to write a book, it should be about how to "get more for less." Instead, I find myself writing about what some people would call "a softer subject" and one with a particularly narrow scope. It is measuring human behaviours via KBIs.

There is a simple reason for choosing this topic. It is the bit that makes the difference.

My career has taken me across multiple industries and geography and has given me deep and insightful experience of when things go well and when they do not. This experience is both from a day-to-day operations point of view and also during change or large-scale transformations.

Luckily, I managed to spot a pattern (unluckily - it was a late discovery!), and I have had the time, space, and opportunity to reflect deeply on these experiences, and then to research and cross-reference them with multiple external sources. From this research, we are able to determine a hypothesis to focus on. With this hypothesis, I then looked deeper into the linkage between behaviours, culture, and outcomes. This research was then linked back to the real-life experiences of myself and many other leaders.

As you can see already, there are lots of links that have been made already, and as you go through this initiative, you will undoubtedly make more of your own. It is amazing that all of these links keep backing up the hypothesis and not raising concerns or issues with it.

The hypothesis is as follows and is expanded from our earlier logic.

If you...

- Believe that "You get what you measure" is true
- Believe that consistent behaviours define your Culture
- Believe that Culture is critical in achieving your Purpose
- Have behaviours that support your Purpose and Culture
- Observe and measure these behaviours as KBIs
- Lead by example to role model the chosen behaviours

- Capture and report on behaviours using KBIs
- Reward people that role model the chosen behaviours
- Track how these behaviours become dominant
- .... then you win!

So, how did I arrive at this?

At the centre of my life, there has been a point of gravity that has pulled me towards solving problems and fixing things. Growing up in a rural location where almost everything seemed to be worn out or broken, the ability to fix things was a daily skill. Curiosity, basic handyman skills, and learning to think differently were critical to both stave off boredom, and to enable daily life to happen with as little drama as possible. As a teenager and while still at school, I helped out in the family greengrocer shop and became much more useful in sorting out something that had gone wrong rather than following the day-to-day routines. I would shuffle around with a huffing and puffing attitude full of "Why does this even need to be done"? I couldn't understand why things were clearly sub-optimal, but people just did them anyway and then did them again the next day. Madness.

After I left school and moved into real employment (i.e. where you actually get paid!), a similar pattern emerged. As a junior employee, naturally, my ability to influence was low, and even when I had the opportunity to call out an issue and suggest how it might be improved, it was typically met with "yeah, a nice idea," but things rarely changed. I could not understand why.

Later on, when I bought my first car (an absolute lemon), it gave me a relentless source of things to fix, and I loved it. I didn't need approval to fix the car; my only constraints were time and money, both of which I now had a little of. I remember becoming slightly disappointed when it would finally make a journey of 10 miles without some sort of failure. By this time, I was working on a delivery truck taking wine and spirits into London pubs. We had lots of issues with routes, timing, and access. It was super frustrating for me and was a dependable topic for the drivers to moan about at the greasy spoon cafe on the way into the city every morning. I would talk with the drivers about some of the problems, and how maybe some of them could be fixed, but I could never seem to get strong support to give them a go. By making a regular pest of myself back in the office with the same thoughts, I was eventually asked to help replan a few of the routes. I'm sure this was more from the "let's keep him quiet for a bit" angle rather than a "maybe this will work" angle, but I relished the chance to help fix things for all the drivers, the customers and of course, me. The changes and solutions did indeed improve things, nothing earth-shattering, but incremental types of improvement. The drivers liked it, and positive feedback even started to come from the customers. What started out as a side-project then grew into a larger replanning of all the routes. This initiative grew further again into a proper project to computerise the entire route planning activity. More success, which then led me into a role in the company data centre and eventually to lead the data centre day-to-day operations. If I wasn't before, I was now totally hooked on solving problems.

Having an inquisitive mind, some freshly acquired computing skills, and a passion for fixing things was working well for me. I moved to a role in a larger corporation and followed a similar path. Although my skillset and experience were growing fast, I started to have a few setbacks. I learned (the hard way) that computerisation of broken processes was not a good idea. It turns out that automating a bad process just gave a quicker delivery of a bad outcome. This was not something that I wanted to be famous for. I needed another way to fix things. To achieve this, my tactic was to start to look at things from a process perspective rather than the usual systems or data perspective. This approach opened up a rich vein of success and quickly became my go-to tactic for pragmatically understanding what was going on and then determining a better way of working. I was now becoming experienced at using both Process and Systems based techniques to solve problems. However, something was still missing. I was starting to realise there was still at least one more perspective that was needed. I started to understand that the People component was not in my thinking.

You may have heard the phrase "People, Process, Systems." I think the sequence of these words is deliberate and important. Firstly, think People, then Process, then finally make the Systems fit - not the other way around.

It then dawned on me that my learning curve had been the other way around. "Systems, Process, People." Whoops.

In retrospect, this was not the end of the world, but I must admit that it was far from ideal. I think as long as you eventually get all three into the mix and balanced appropriately, then good things (magic) can happen. This challenge is that most of us still have a bias towards Process and Systems and we end up forcing the People component to fit. This is one of the main reasons why a lot of change fails. We need the People component first, but we also need all three otherwise the magic never happens.

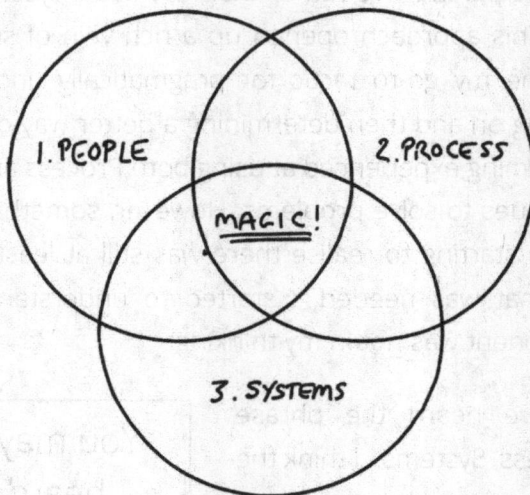

In my naivety, I had always assumed that people actually wanted things to be fixed and that change and business improvement were positive experiences for people. People would surely be looking forward to change and things being better. Why would I need to consider or design the People part of the change? Won't they grab it with both hands and just find a way to do it and make the most of it? As I am sure you are aware, in reality, it seems most people don't.

Eventually, I did find a way to bring some of the People aspects into view with an emerging discipline called Business Architecture.

This practice blended characteristics like 'Accountability' and 'Capability' with Processes, Systems, Data, and KPIs. It helped me understand and start to codify the people impact of solving the problem and the degree of changes they might face. Business Architecture does indeed give a broad view of what makes the organisation tick. Maybe I now had the holy trinity of People, Process, Systems? Of course not. It was a token gesture, a tick in the box to help me convince people (including myself) that there had been some consideration of people in the design. There was still very little in my Skillset or Toolset on how to actually design the human part of the change.

One activity that did seem to help a bit more was to stay close to 'where the work was done.' This tactic allowed me to gain a solid understanding of the pain that problems were causing for people and then gauge the energy levels of the workforce to 'want to' solve the problem. I was starting to pick up on the notion of willingness to change, which helped me focus energy and commitment on what was needed to follow through with potential solutions and improvements. This tactic to 'do work on the frontline' is now a common concept, and its importance and value should not be underestimated. My insistence to get my hands dirty and experience operations (not just watch it) helped with both my credibility and also the success and sustainability of the change.

This tactic of keeping close to the front line and thinking across People, Process, and Systems became an important technique for me in delivering change. It was not a one-off; it proved successful across many organisations, regardless of the business sector or

> I learned that humans are predictable regardless of company, country, or industry.

geography. I learned that humans are predictable regardless of company, country, or industry. But still, this was not enough; things still never felt as easy as they should have been.

On a parallel track, another nagging feeling I had was with 'Change Management.' This obviously People-oriented profession has become mainstream over the past couple of decades. I totally support it, and I believe in it, or at least, I want to believe in it. It makes total sense and should help add more strength to the People side of change, right? In reality, though, I still had an uneasiness that something was missing, and I could sense that others felt the same way too. Why was there such buy-in towards the 'Change Management' concept, but seemingly such little tangible benefit as a result? I understood the models from Kotter and ADKAR and followed them as closely as most people do. I also understood the evidence and facts about how much change fails and the reasons for it. However, there was still a disconnect between what these models recommend on 'how to make change stick' and what was actually happening in projects under the banner of Change Management. In projects 'post-implementation reviews,' there was a consistent theme: we should communicate more, or we should manage the stakeholder better. It was hardly ever 'perfect - we nailed it.' Why do we need so many resources and so much energy to change?

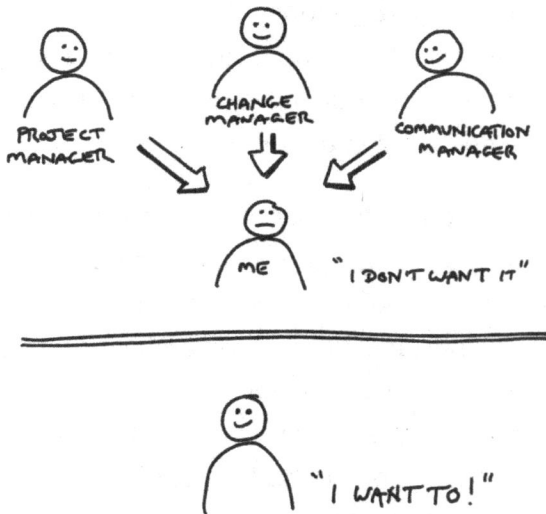

In the diagram above, I am showing two scenarios. In the one at the top, you can see some people performing roles in a typical project. If the person (me in this case) does not want to change, then the project is destined for some tough times, possibly even failure. In the one underneath, you can see an individual who 'wants' to change. Even though there is no project team - there is a chance this person will find a way to find improvements and discover a better way of working. Of course, some projects need a team to deliver the outcome as a lot of coordination of specialist resources and sequenced events need to take place. But some do not. We can often find a fully resourced project team in place for what could be done by somebody using their initiative - if they 'wanted' to. I could now start to see that the People component can never be the 'tick the box' part of things - it is the main game.

Make no mistake, it is the same for day-to-day operations as well. Some employees only get the Must-do work done when they have people on their backs (e.g. supervisors, customers, colleagues). Other employees contribute above-and-beyond and get through an amazing amount of Could-do work without any visibility to others, let alone encouragement or direction.

The cornerstone of the resistance to change lies within someone's Mindset. I'm not proposing that we don't need Project Managers, Change Managers, and Communications Managers; these resources play important roles in coordinating large-scale and complex change and transformation. I'm not saying that we need to create a role of Mindset Manager either. For small incremental change, maybe only one person's Mindset needs to be in the right place; for bigger change, then more Mindsets. Now we start to understand the sliding scale of "the bigger the change - the less successful it will probably be."

Let's step back for a moment and talk more about People Capability, which loosely falls into three distinct buckets: Toolset, Skillset, and Mindset.

Toolset: the knowledge and experience of using external (non-human) devices, equipment, computer software, or data, etc.

Skillset: the knowledge and experience of using methodologies, processes, standards, techniques, tactics, and codified ways of working.

Mindset: the knowledge and experience of using thinking, reasoning, and decision-making actions.

Let's go back to recap what I had learned so far. Initially, my ways of working were focused on using a specific Toolset to fix things. For me, the tool of choice was technology. The analogy of 'when you only have a hammer, everything looks like a nail' was totally relevant for me. For every problem that I found, for every improvement that I could propose, I would use technology as the way to solve the problem. In some cases, this was probably a good option; in other cases, a similar outcome may have been possible using non-technology-based options, and in the remaining cases, using technology was definitely not the right way to go.

As I started to recognise that maybe technology was not the only way, I began to look at how other people and other projects were able to make improvements and solve problems. I noticed that a lot of benefit was coming from focusing on 'how' work was being done, not just on 'what' equipment was being utilised. The discipline of focusing on the 'how' was called Process Management.

By learning, adopting, and employing Process Management methods and techniques, I was able to balance my work by now using Skillsets. This focus and improvement on 'how' people worked were typically achieved through simplification (less skill needed) or standardisation (easier to become skilled if the routine is more predictable and stable). The success rate, especially in the larger projects and "transformation" type initiatives, was much improved. It was much better than the "80% failure" statistic, but the full potential still seemed out of reach, and there was always a feeling that something valuable had been left on the table.

I then finally became aware of how Mindset can trump both Toolset and Skillset. If only I had figured this out in the reverse order! After experiencing for myself how this worked, I went back into my memories of all the initiatives I had worked on before, the roles

I had, and the teams I had worked with and in. I caught up with old colleagues and replayed the key moments with them, cross-referencing them with where the successes were stronger and where we had missed the mark. The correlation was watertight. Every time there had been an emphasis on Mindset (either deliberately or by chance), the outcome was highly positive, and great things happened. Where Mindset was pushed to the back of the queue or simply not considered, the outcomes were poor, and sometimes even the initiative was cancelled.

A lot of this backstory so far has been in the context of change. Don't worry, all these points are just as relevant for day-to-day operations, and they will all lead us to the same place. Even day-to-day operations are full of change, maybe more at the micro level with something as simple as a phone call or a customer query. From a behaviour viewpoint, the way I react to an unexpected phone call is just as natural and important as the way I react to accepting a more significant change to my routines, systems, or my role accountability.

In one of my more recent roles, and with the uneasy warmth that comes with being confident that you think you are good at what you do, I was literally stunned and shell-shocked to realise that I had missed the most important aspect of 'change' altogether. I was working on an initiative to train the entire company workforce (around 6,000 people) in Problem-Solving skills. Our small team consisted of a diverse mix of experts from the fields of Lean, Six Sigma, Training, Change Management, Communications, and of course, Problem Solving. The Problem-Solving courses that the team built were absolutely solid, the best I had ever seen. The workforce loved the courses, there was even a waiting list to join them. They loved the tools, and the feedback from attendees after the course was simply fantastic, 5 stars all the way. But in terms of impact - little changed. The end result was that we had taken a few days out of people's working week for them to attend the courses, and when they returned to their workplace, they mostly carried on doing exactly what they were doing before. What had we missed? Why didn't we shift the needle? We did a review with a forensic level of detail. What were we asked to do? What did we do? What happened? The investigation revealed a single standout truth. People didn't want to solve their problems; they didn't want to fix things. In hindsight, it feels obvious, and I am confident that when you read ahead - you will say, 'Yeah - of course, duh!'. The fact remains; this was a smart, streetwise, experienced group of professionals with a superb leadership team and support, and we were all blindsided.

The bottom line was that if you don't want to do it, you can always find a reason why it won't get done. If you avoid it long enough, there will always be another reason that you use for why the task never got done. The ultimate reason being, "I just ran out of time."

> The bottom line was that if you don't want to do it, you can always find a reason why it won't get done.

After discovering what we had missed, we went back to the drawing board and redesigned our courses to focus on cultivating a Mindset of problem-solving. It was a significant risk, a gamble, but based on the investigation and thorough feedback, we had a good feeling about it. We received positive support, advice, and guidance from our internal colleagues, including HR

Development Managers and Change Managers. They thought that this concept was somewhat unconventional but completely feasible and definitely worth trying. This attempt wasn't entirely a random "shot in the dark" for us, but we were going into uncharted territory. One fortunate event for us was when we made a discovery that became a defining source of inspiration for us. We became aware of the work of Mr. Shigeo Shingo. For reference, Mr. Shingo was at the centre of the famously effective and efficient Toyota Production System and a key contributor to defining the Toyota culture.

The Shingo model and approach had originally been used by our team some time before as a way to help give Process Management some wider context and linkage. It shows how processes (note: called 'systems' for some reason in the Shingo model) connect to behaviours, culture, and results. This was aligned with our hunch that Mindset was really the key to unlocking the power of our smart 6000-strong workforce. The technique of measuring behaviours and their link to culture from the Shingo model was now centre stage for us. The rest is, as they say, history. The new courses now had very little content on "how" to solve problems. Instead, they focused on behaviours and "why" solving problems was a good thing. The title of the initiative was called 'Self-Healing'. The quality of the courses was up to the team's typical high standard, and as expected, so was the feedback after the courses.

We started to track the impacts again, and this time the results were remarkable. The grassroots groundswell of people solving their own problems that emerged was nothing less than tectonic. Prior to this program, it is fair to say that the organisation had developed a sense of 'learned helplessness'. There was a 150-strong team of dedicated

....

'fixers,' and the attitude of the workforce was that it was the fixers' job to fix stuff, not theirs. Clearly not a sustainable situation.

After this new set of courses had been delivered, and as the snowball of 'Self-Healing' started to gain momentum, we were able to reduce this 150-strong team (the majority of which were highly paid Lean Six Sigma Black Belts, and even a handful of Master Black Belts) to less than 20. More problems than ever were being solved, and faster. All business performance targets were surpassed. Output was more than doubled, the overall cost was reduced, and customer satisfaction and team engagement also increased. These statistics were repeated again the next year. And yes, that's a 100%+ improvement on top of a 100%+ improvement - with an even lower cost base.

It is, of course, naive to believe that this success was all down to the content of a few training courses. Many other things made up the full picture of what was going on. But nevertheless, it was evident that this huge nudge on Mindset was a critical component in uniting the organisation and unleashing the dormant capability that had been sitting there all along. It has to be said that a key part of the success was that it was owned and driven by the CEO and his team. As a result of this ownership, the concept became infused into the habits of the organisation.

And so, the link between Mindset and Behaviours had been tested in an exceptionally challenging workplace scenario where other methods had already failed, and it was found to be strong, positive, and consistent. It was the game changer that we needed.

This link between Behaviours, Mindset, and results is important for us not to forget.

In the last few years, I have conducted several targeted experiments on the topic of Mindset, Behaviours, and KBIs. These experiments have been targeted to define, detect, and measure the impacts of the KBI concept and determine its value. The results of these experiments provided me with the proof points and evidence needed to be confident in the effectiveness and sustainability of this approach. I now firmly believe that KBIs are a game changer, and their impact is both wide and deep.

> Today, when I discuss KBIs with leaders, the reaction is consistent. Initially, there is surprise that something so obvious seems to have been missed.

Today, when I discuss KBIs with leaders, the reaction is consistent. Initially, there is surprise that something so obvious seems to have been missed. Then there is usually some energy and urgency to do something about it, followed by some reflection over concerns on 'how' it could be done. Implementing KBIs can be challenging if you don't know where to start, or what path to follow. This book is designed to provide you with the tools and guidance needed to implement KBIs effectively. It outlines a prescribed process, including workshops and meetings that show the way. These are guidelines and can be used or swapped out for activities that are more familiar to your organisation. If you or your organisation has different methods for achieving the same results, then please use them. Maintaining a recognisable home-grown approach can help build trust and speed up engagement, which is beneficial.

It's worth noting that this book focuses on a specific subset of Mindset, namely Behaviours, and how to measure them. There are many other elements of Mindset, and a lot has been written about them. However, the measurement of Behaviours seems to be a relatively overlooked aspect so far. If you're new to the field of Organisational Psychology and Mindset Improvement, this book provides a good starting point, with no prior knowledge required. However, as you embark on this journey, it will be beneficial for you to broaden your understanding of what motivates people and gain experience on how to leverage that knowledge to improve performance.

To save you from the same fate as myself, I urge you to take your time and digest this book slowly. I wouldn't recommend skimming through it and bursting into action. Let the concept soak in, simmer for a while. Talk to your colleagues about it, see which parts resonate the most with them, and in the context of your organisation. The book provides everything you need to bring KBIs to life, but running your own experiments, collecting local sentiment, and tailoring the approach to suit organisational preferences and leadership styles will pay off.

SECTION 2
What Are KBIs?

Even with what little you have read so far, you probably already know more than most people you are likely to discuss this with. While traditional Key Performance Indicators (KPIs) have been the go-to metric for measuring organisational performance for decades, they have limitations that KBIs can help address. We are about to delve deeper into the concept of KBIs, how they differ from KPIs, and why they can be more effective for not only measuring current performance but also predicting how strong the organisation will be going forward.

What are Key Behaviour Indicators?

KBIs are metrics used to measure employee behaviour and attitudes in the workplace. Unlike KPIs, which are typically focused on measuring outcomes such as revenue, profit, or efficiency, KBIs provide insights into the mindset of your employees and how well they are set up to achieve the company's purpose, objectives, and targets. For example, a KBI can measure the level of employee readiness to solve a complex problem.

KBIs measure behaviours that lead towards a wide range of outcomes or characteristics, with some examples below:

- Employee Engagement
- Levels of Trust & Loyalty
- Confidence & Courage
- Productivity & Efficiency
- Accountability & Ownership
- Quality of Work, Customer Service
- Being competitive, Winning for Customers

- Reducing Complexity / Striving for Simplicity
- Safety, Compliance, Resilience
- Communication & Collaboration

While KPIs and KBIs are both used to measure performance, they differ in one important way.

> KPIs are typically focused on factual, tangible, and quantifiable metrics.

KPIs tell you what happened. They are always historical. 'Performance' is in the past tense. KPIs are typically focused on factual, tangible, and quantifiable metrics. Something must have occurred for a KPI to exist.

KBIs, however, look forward and can predict what will happen. They focus on employee actions that will impact outcomes which will then feed into KPIs at a later date. Because KBIs report on what behaviours currently have, and will have, they show you where you are going.

Another key difference is that while KPIs are typically quantitative metrics, KBIs can be both quantitative and qualitative. For example, a KPI might measure the percentage of customer complaints resolved within a certain timeframe, while a KBI might measure the quality of the interaction between the employee and the customer during the resolution process.

The specific KBIs that are most relevant and useful to your organisation will depend on your purpose, goals, culture, and industry. For instance, a manufacturing company might be biased towards KBIs that optimise the efficiency of its production line, while a retail company might lean towards KBIs to optimise the quality of customer service.

Why is this important?

There are several areas where KBIs can be more effective than KPIs. Here are a few examples:

- KBIs provide deep insights into employee engagement
- KBIs identify areas for improvement
- KBIs drive responsible change
- KBIs are more predictive than KPIs
- KBIs provide a new angle of insight

We will delve deeper into these in a moment. Before we do that, I want to share one of the key moments that made a huge difference for me in understanding the benefits of KBIs. It came from the following proverb.

"The church is near, but the road is icy,
the bar is far away, but I
will walk carefully."

Let's dissect this for a moment. It might be the right thing to go to church, but I have found a reason why I can't, so I won't. Conversely, it might not be the right thing to go to the bar, and there is a much greater obstacle in my way, but I have a reason to get there, so I will!

Ultimately, I don't want to go to church. I want to go to the bar.

With KBIs, you can capture people's intent. The KPI would report back on how many people ended up in the bar, and how many in the church - but it won't help you understand why. By carefully selecting the right KBI, you can understand why there are (most probably) more people in the bar.

By defining, sharing, and measuring key behaviours in your organisation, you start to exert a tiny force on the way people think. Think of it as a small tugboat nudging the bow of an oil tanker. If that small but consistent force is applied for long enough, you get the oil tanker going in a completely different direction with minimal fuss or drama. Over time, this tiny force changes people's habits and provides them with the internal reasons to find a way to do the right thing as shaped and encouraged by a small set of KBIs. This fundamental fact about the mechanics of KBIs provides the foundation for most of the benefits. Now, let's get back into that list and see where this mechanic is woven into each example.

KBIs provide deep insights into employee engagement. By using KBIs, you can gain an understanding of underlying and unseen factors that are impacting outcomes. For example, a KPI may show a high rate of absenteeism among employees, but it does not explain why. By measuring a KBI, you could start to see 'why' the team does not want to come to work. For example, a KBI on 'promoting our purpose' would tell you how well the organisation's purpose is understood. It would also inform you of how connected your team is to it by noticing how often the 'purpose' is used to guide decision-making or action. Why would this KBI be insightful? Typically, when you dig into widespread absenteeism, you find a predictable set of reasons, e.g.

- I don't know if what I do matters.
- I'm not valued.
- There is no point. Why bother?

By tactically having a KBI on 'promoting our purpose,' you can make the link to these typical issues. Until your team truly understands the organisation's purpose, how can they possibly feel valued or see the point in why they should go out of their way to do anything more than the bare minimum? Maybe it is better to take the day off after all? This difference in approach is subtle, but the impact and insights will go far beyond the specific concern of absenteeism; it flows into everything that everyone does. As such, it will also generate positive impacts in quality control, customer service, productivity, and so on.

KBIs can be used to identify areas for improvement. There are many tools and skills (e.g., Lean, Six Sigma, Customer Journey

Mapping, Process Mining) that provide ways to scientifically wanalyse what happened and how a better outcome could have been achieved if it was done differently. These tools are great, and they should be continued to be used. However, KBIs can provide an extra dimension that these tools and skills cannot. For instance, let's say that a process has not been changed, nor have the tools, systems, data, or even the roles of the people who follow the process. If we had a KBI that promoted innovation, we might be able to find a way to improve something that we didn't even know needed improving. A KBI of 'Asks what if?' would give encouragement and permission to the team to come up with ideas on how things could be improved. There's no such thing as a bad idea, but if they never see the light of day, who will ever know? I have seen this happen in both a day-to-day operations context and during change programmes. It causes a complete flip in the conversations of the team on the front line. A typical conversation between workmates of "Hey, we should do this" would usually be followed by a "hmmm, it'll never work" reply. The dialogue flipped to "What if we did this?" followed by "And then, what if we did that?" The conversation would rapidly progress, draw others in, and more often than not, there would eventually be a consensus among the group on what could be done to make something better. Even if a consensus couldn't be reached, the seeds have now been sown. Sooner or later, someone will come up with a way to make an

> If we had a KBI that promoted innovation, we might be able to find a way to improve something that we didn't even know needed improving.

improvement. Therefore, it would only be a matter of time before an improvement actually occurred. What a great mindset to have embedded in your team.

KBIs can drive responsible change within an organisation. I will assume that you have a KPI in your organisation that relates to safety, probably something like "lost time injury". Imagine the power of a KBI that looks forward and provides predictability on whether you will have more or fewer safety-related incidents. For example, suppose a KBI measures the level of belief that employees have in the safety standards and their intent to 'be safe' and protect their well-being as well as their teammates. If we increase the level of this belief, adherence to following the safety standards is more likely to improve, and the number of safety incidents will be lower.

Let's have a crack at a KBI called 'Keeps Our Mates Safe'. This KBI would measure how instinctive it is for every team member to be on the lookout for everyone else's safety, physically or mentally. This changes the world of 'safety' from tick-the-box activities into a deep and real desire to ensure that everyone can go home today with the same level of well-being that they turned up with this morning (or maybe even better). You would be signalling that you want to see teammates calling out to each other when they may be in danger. Over time, this becomes a habit, and the respect that people have (especially as incidents get prevented) for each other rises. This habit hardens, and the organisation becomes recognised for its safety culture. It seems a difficult path to get here with KPIs, but for KBIs - it just happens, and then snowballs onwards. I have seen this in action, and when an external safety audit was performed, the organisation received a glowing report on its safety culture and the unprompted and unsupervised level of care that all employees and management had for each other.

KBIs bring confidence. Because KBIs are more predictive than KPIs and remain stable even when many other variables change, we can continue to move at speed as we are assured of how we will react. It is said that 'speed is the only competitive advantage'. The insight we can create through KBIs gives us confidence in how our team will work and overcome the challenges of today and also into the future. This confidence enables speed. If we were to look at this from another perspective for a moment, let's say 'our close circle of friends'. The reason we keep these friends as friends is because of who they are; we know what we can expect from them in any situation. Even when crazy things happen in their lives, we can still see 'them' in the way that they deal with chaos. You would have heard the phrase "Hire for mindset". This is a good call as it helps predict what type of contribution you will get regardless of what else happens. For example, if a delivery into your warehouse does not happen, an employee with low engagement and care factor might just wait for the next delivery while all the downstream processes start to become impacted. However, a proactive and engaged employee (i.e. one with the right Mindset) would signal to the downstream teams that there has been an issue while also trying to secure delivery of the expected goods at the earliest possible opportunity. Which would be the most useful to you? There are no differences in skills or tools, just attitude. Will you get the best outcome by measuring the number of missed deliveries or the behaviour and mindset of your employees in how they would deal with it (and by default - any other issue)? A single KBI can therefore replace many KPIs. They can provide early warning signs of potential problems before they even happen.

KBIs provide you with a new angle of insight into your workforce capability that has been missing. There is a well-trodden path in understanding your strength of human capital in terms of the 'Skillset' that they have: training, certification, years in the role, and so on. These skillset parameters can have a KPI, for example, 'percentage of mechanics that have worked for 1 year post certification on internal combustion engines'. Psychometric analysis can also have a KPI, for example - how many 'conceptual thinkers' do you have. It is also easy to understand the capability of the organisation that is supported through the 'Toolset'. Again, this can have a KPI, for example, 'age of laptops'. So, if we analyse our KPIs with the aim to increase the performance of the team, we would think we need to train them and give them better equipment, right? Well, that won't hurt at all. But what are we not getting? Why are there so many examples of where the team with less training and old equipment still outperforms a team with the best of everything? Why do we see the football players with the best equipment, the best ground, the best nutritionists, and the best facilities deliver on-pitch performances that leave the fans cold? The answer to why this happens is, of course, in the realm of 'Mindset'. It's why we now see psychologists on the staff at these larger football clubs. The bottom line is that if the team wants to win, they will find a way to win or at least make the supporters proud of their efforts to do so. If the team can't be bothered or maybe is only bothered about themselves, then no amount of training, tools, or tactics will get you across the line. How can you tell where the 'Mindset' of the team is if you don't measure it?

Let's consider 'value' for a moment. The value of an organisation is often assessed by its share price. We understand that this share price is partly based on the company's performance to date, but it is usually more heavily weighted on the expectations for the company going forward. The question is, "How much value will be created in the future?" Strong KPI metrics tell you that you performed well, but they do not always equate to continued success and an increase in your share price. In fact, you often see the opposite, once super strong results have been delivered, the share price can take a dip - the market is assuming that the best has been and gone, and it's now downhill. So, the share price is more closely linked to how well the organisation is positioned to win in the future and how much value will be created. Some of this is linked to the brand value and the known culture and capability of the organisation to overcome the known and unknown challenges that could be around the corner.

Hopefully, we can therefore agree that measuring history (the

KPI) is only a small part of the picture. To get the full picture and a better idea of the future, we need to measure it, and our team's behaviour is a great place to start.

Measuring human behaviour provides a strategic advantage in predicting future performance. If you are confident about the mindset of your employees, how well they understand the company's purpose, how well they trust their leaders and each other, how courageous and determined they are to overcome issues and find ways to make it better, then the company has a much higher chance of meeting its objectives and being successful, no matter what challenges arise. What if I were to ask you "Are your competitors in the same place?" Can you see your advantage?

> Measuring human behaviour provides a strategic advantage in predicting future performance.

So, we have talked a little about behaviours now. I imagine you have an idea of what I mean by it, but it is most likely that the people around all have slightly different views on what is meant by behaviour. To get us all aligned, and for the purpose of this book, we should settle on a single definition of what behaviour is. This is not as simple as it sounds, section 5 is dedicated to providing more explanation, but we will deal with the first building block now. There are many variations of this description across academia, white papers, psychometric studies, and so on. For simplicity and ease of use, we shall use a simple short one and reference back to it several times. I am sure this will be wrong in the eyes of some people, but it is useful, easy to explain, and thus it is more likely for us to align on it.

A behaviour is:

> *"a detectable human action*
> *in reaction to a trigger."*

For clarity, any external stimulus (to the person) is a potential trigger. For example, a certain behaviour can be triggered by an issue, a conversation, a scheduled event, another person's actions, an email, a phone call, a customer enquiry, and so on.

Our behaviours come from a number of different places. Our most raw and primal set are our Genetic Behaviours, these are embedded deep within us. The "Fight or Flight" reaction is one example that is hard-wired into us. It helps protect us and keep us safe. We will not measure this type of behaviour.

Another set of behaviours becomes ingrained in us over time from our social environment. An example of this could be around the social norms of our personal culture or our family, e.g. "respect for our elders." These different social cultures are the sum of our environmentally driven behaviours on what it takes to be 'in' with a certain group. We feel compelled to behave in these ways, although we are often unsure why. These behaviours drift over time, as we ourselves drift in what we believe in, and the social environment we find ourselves in, or perhaps want to be in.

An interesting example could be the difference between living in a very rural setting where your neighbour is miles away, or very urban where they live a few meters away. The rural situation may encourage behaviours that prioritise mutual trust and respect between you both. Deep down, you know that one day something bad could happen, and you will need that person to come to the rescue, and you accept the vice versa of this understanding. Alternatively, living in a dense urban environment may encourage you to keep your distance and seek privacy from the person who lives just a few meters away from you. In this situation, you may feel there is competition for space and resources. It is best to protect what you have rather than share it (or worse - have it taken from you). Your environment is influencing your behaviours and habits. We won't measure this type of behaviour either.

The last main grouping of behaviours are those that we have learned and refined over our lifetime and come from our personal experiences, the knowledge we accumulate from the world around us, and what makes us feel good. It is this set of behaviours that has the most neuroplasticity and where we have the most opportunity to intervene and change them. We should aim to measure these types of behaviours.

By focusing and working on this last set of behaviours, by explaining why some are important to the organisation, and why we want to measure them - we are bringing transparency about a mental blueprint for our organisation that we want to move towards. This is far more influential than any policy, standard operating procedure, or approval committee could ever be. We can become confident that our teams are doing the right thing, all day, every day, no matter what challenges appear in front of them. There is an element of futureproofing here as well. For example, imagine a brand-new scenario that could not possibly have a playbook or policy on how to manage it. It could still be handled well if the team has the guardrails on behaviours to help them make a great call and get through it. Maybe in hindsight, they might not do the 'perfect' thing, but it will be an honest effort to do the right thing, and that will mean a lot to all the people involved. I'm sure you can think of a customer service situation where things were stacked against the employee, but after they stepped up and did what they could, the customer was delighted. Even though the result may not have been ideal, the customer still felt compelled to post it on social media about what a great job had been done for them. The chances are that this example was driven more by a personal behavioural trait of the employee, and not by a policy or procedure document that they had memorised. No policy, no standard operating procedure, no process, but a great outcome. How powerful is that?

Now, let's imagine that this was not a 'one-off'. Let us imagine that this employee is consistent with their behaviour towards all customers in all situations. Not only that, let's imagine that their behaviour has rubbed off on the team around them. The whole team has some common habits when they face these tough situations.

A critical point then, what would you call "consistently repeated behaviours"?

How about **Culture?**   Bingo!

This is not suggesting that KBIs will (or should) brainwash your workforce into mindless lemmings. There are thousands of other attributes to a person's personality that will allow their unique qualities to shine through and for diversity to be maintained. A handful of well-selected KBIs will give enough of a framework to enable a tangible Culture to be defined and moved towards, while still allowing people's characters to be unrestricted.

By carefully selecting a set of KBIs that are aligned and in tune with the company's purpose, goals, and values, you can now get both this tangible definition for your desired organisation Culture AND a way to measure it. An interesting side point: have you ever put somebody on the spot and asked them to describe their organisation's culture? The chances are that they would have struggled to clearly articulate it. KBIs will help by providing a framework to describe and share what the desired organisation Culture is. It gives clarity to customers, employees, and even 'the market' about what the company stands for and, therefore, will ultimately support and sustain the Brand that you are trying to be famous for. Remember that organisational value (and share price) is driven as much by Brand as it is by the bottom line.

> An interesting side point: have you ever put somebody on the spot and asked them to describe their organisation's culture?

KPIs are, and will always be important, but we need to understand that this is in a similar way that history books are important. By understanding what happened, we can make more informed decisions about what we do next. History has a habit of repeating itself until there is a deliberate intervention to take a different path. If the definition of insanity is 'doing the same thing and expecting a different result,' then finding a way to 'not do the same thing' must be both sane and worth it.

KBIs will show you how well set up you are going forward and if your organisation has the mindset to take a different (and better) path to get the desired outcome. KBIs are also the glue that connects your KPIs to the company's Purpose, Mission, Strategic Goals, Values, Culture, and Brand.

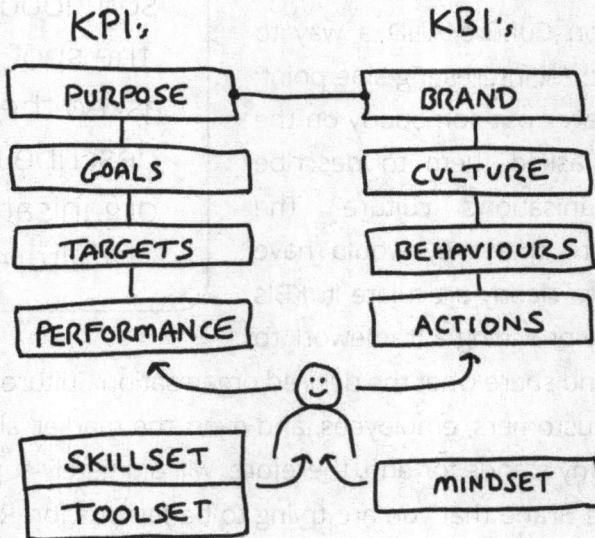

The diagram above illustrates my belief about how the connection between an employee and the two outcomes of Purpose and Brand stack up. You can see how the KPI stack can be quite mechanical in linking practical Skills and Tools to Performance that contributes to achieving the organisation's Purpose. With KBIs, you can see the pathway to Culture and Brand. The Purpose and the Brand have to be complementary, so at the top level, they will hopefully become integrated, but until then, they are on different paths. Having both hands on the steering wheel (or stacks) gives better control over the direction, enabling you to manage bumps in the road and manoeuvre around obstacles that get in your way.

The following sections in this book will take you on a journey where you will gain a more thorough understanding of KBIs, how to select them, how to implement them, and how to secure the long-term strategic advantage that they can provide.

SECTION 3
Getting Started

There is a critical moment in launching this initiative in your organisation that we should address early.

Until the CEO is determined to lead this initiative from the front, and until the senior team is 100% on board - DO NOT LAUNCH.

I am expecting that you will need to go through a process to bring this concept up to the senior team, or maybe you are one of the senior team planning to share this with your peers. This initiative will find both supporters and detractors of the concept. As a result, getting the senior team 100% on board may take some time, and it may need to come back to the table more than once before you get the unified support that is needed. This is OK. I recommend you wait and get unified support rather than getting half of the team supporting you and the other half trying to pull the rug from under you.

There really is no wriggle room here. For KBIs to be successful, they need to be adopted with unrelenting diligence by the senior team before they can be released and cascaded through the organisation. A passive "Yeah - OK" won't be enough. There needs to be a pact across the senior team where everyone is totally invested, with no lip service being paid and no "let's see how it goes." Agreement and involvement of every member of the team are critical. With the KBI initiative, leaders cannot choose to behave differently from the behaviour coached and encouraged in the workforce. Doing this would cause trust to be impacted, and KBIs will end up causing more harm than good. This approach is very much 'do as I do, not as I say,' not the other way around.

> The concept of KBIs works best when it permeates the entire organisation.

This initiative should not be piloted in a corner of the organisation to see how it goes. Your teams interact all day, every day. By quarantining this initiative into a specific department or geography, you are creating a point of difference and it will create some friction that you are better off without. The concept of KBIs works best when it permeates the entire organisation. Remember the notion that behaviours build culture. If you have two or more flavours of preferred behaviours, then you develop a split personality in your culture.

Luckily, the KBI concept is usually a relatively easy sell to the senior team, but it does take them some time to let it sink in. There can even be a degree of embarrassment that they did not initiate or think of it themselves, as it seems so obvious once you reflect on it for a while. Typically, a group that operates at this top level would be able to see that the massive potential positives in this initiative far outweigh any debatable negatives. By the way, after years and years of looking at this, I have yet to capture a real negative of this concept, there must be some somewhere. If you discover some, please share them with me!

Getting back to the thoughts of the senior team for a moment. One of the objectives of a senior team is to manage the operational performance of their functions or teams and to align their resources and efforts to achieve the strategic objectives of the organisation, so that it achieves its purpose. Another objective is to lead the people that report to them, to nurture and develop them, and to inspire them to be better and achieve their full potential. This latter objective can sometimes be difficult for some senior execs to get a firm grip on. KBIs can be a useful tactic in helping with this part of their role.

If after sharing this initiative with the senior team, you find that the concept does not resonate with them at all, I would say this is unusual. The most common response is usually "tell me more." If you come up against fierce resistance to this concept, then it may be time for you to think again about what the organisation is trying to do, how it is trying to do it, and if that sits well with you. Let's hope you are a long way from this situation.

Let's assume that you have gained resounding support from the senior team to proceed with this initiative. In Section 8, we step through a series of events that provide a pathway to introducing KBIs into the business. Throughout that section, there are activities and milestones for engagement and communication with the wider organisation. The way in which this is done should be subtle and in tune with how these things are typically presented. Don't worry, there is absolutely no need to make a big song and dance about KBIs.

The timeline should be flexible. It is normal for the senior team to take around three months to adopt the concept of KBIs and start to practice the KBIs themselves in a safe environment and to get confident and comfortable enough to release them to the rest of the next layer of the organisation. The optimal technique for gaining this confidence seems to be for the senior team to ask the people around them to help them improve their behaviours (which are aligned with the KBIs) and call out when they exhibit them. Sometimes a deliberate process of using the last 5 minutes of any meeting to reflect on which behaviours were observed in the session helps get the ball rolling. Once this seems to have settled down, then the senior team should ask their team to do the same as they did, and once settled, ask that it is repeated, and so on. Depending on the layers and size of the organisation, this could take 6 months for a Small/Medium-sized company, 12 months (as per the diagram below) for a large single-market corporation, and up to maybe 18 months for a large multinational corporation.

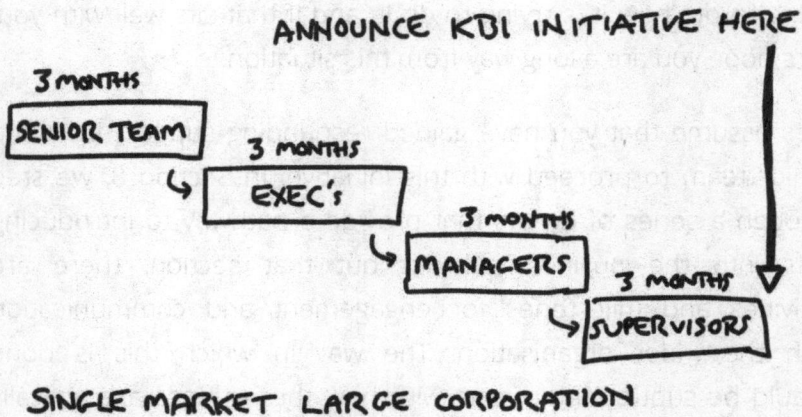

ANNOUNCE KBI INITIATIVE HERE

3 MONTHS
SENIOR TEAM
3 MONTHS
EXEC'S
3 MONTHS
MANAGERS
3 MONTHS
SUPERVISORS

SINGLE MARKET LARGE CORPORATION

Once there is a sense that most of the management levels have some experience with getting and giving feedback on behaviours, then that seems to be the best time to announce the KBI initiative. The published reasoning for this should be that the KBIs will provide support and add some structure to the very informal and ad hoc feedback that had been happening up until then. This usually adds a useful reason for people to be more diligent and disciplined about calling out when the behaviours linked to KBIs are observed.

As you read your way through this book, I encourage you to take notes on the points that resonate with you, especially in relation to the way your organisation functions. Determine options for how you could apply them to the situations in your organisation. Spend some quality time planning how to bring this concept to the key stakeholders in your organisation. Work on your approach to raise awareness and generate the interest it will need.

You cannot start the conversation too early with KBIs, but you can doom it to failure if you start without the correct support and leadership. After you have read this book, you will have a well-rounded understanding of what KBIs are, their power, and how they can provide a strategic advantage to your organisation. You can start doing this yourself by encouraging others around you to call out when they see you behaving in certain ways. It's good to get some experience so that you can share your story when briefing others. Treat it more as an experiment, and definitely not a pilot.

> You cannot start the conversation too early with KBIs, but you can doom it to failure if you start without the correct support and leadership.

SECTION 4
The Limits of KPIs

I am not 'anti-KPI'. I need to say that, as this section does include a fair amount of criticism about them. Coming from a world of business improvement, I recognise that KPIs are essential in understanding if your organisation is better now than it was before. The issue is that KPIs have grown into plague-like proportions and are over-constraining organisations and the workforces inside them.

Let's start by breaking down the three words in 'KPI' with some dictionary definitions.

KEY   - of paramount or crucial importance
PERFORMANCE - how successfully it was performed
INDICATOR   - shows the state or level of something

Let's take a closer look at each of these now.

KEY. This first word seems to be redundant. But it shouldn't be! If I asked you how many KPIs exist in your organisation, you might answer "a few hundred or so." However, you are probably well short of the mark; there are likely to be thousands of them. Surely, not all can be "of paramount or crucial importance"? This prompts me to introduce the concept of removing them, as many as you dare.

A KPI is like a warning light demanding your attention. By having so many alarm bells constantly ringing out across your organisation, it drains the energy of your workforce and shifts the focus from managing operations to "managing the KPI". Which of a hundred KPIs is 'the one' to focus on right now? What if I pick the wrong one? Eventually, with the never-ending dashboard of things to worry about, people become hardened to it, saying, "Yeah, it's been red for a while now." So, what are we actually trying to achieve by having everything as 'key'?

I remember a governance group that worked for years to turn around an organisation and manage a sea of red KPIs into green ones. They drew in more and more resources, took up more and more time; they changed the definitions of some KPIs so they did not need to be red anymore. In the end, they won; they turned the page from red to green - success! But, the organisation was somehow in worse shape than when they had started. Then came the suspicion: "I can't believe everything is green. Someone must be lying to us." The team was sent to check and recheck the KPIs. Everything was true, but the organisation had become dysfunctional and obsessed with managing the KPIs and not caring about the customer. The customer had moved; their expectations were different, and the team did not follow them. They were only focused and constrained with turning red KPIs into green KPIs.

Perhaps your personal performance is gauged more on the KPIs in your objectives than on what you actually do and how you do it. Such an approach makes getting the result at any cost justifiable (behaving negatively becomes acceptable, perhaps even encouraged). Also, it can ignite the start of a toxic employee and if left unchecked - a toxic culture of "Get the results and burn anything to get there".

Any metric is more likely to act as a constraint than an enabler. The more metrics you have - the more burden you are placing on your team and your organisation. Even 'stretch' metrics that set a target higher than is currently being achieved will still put the brakes on something, somewhere, somehow. There is always a price and trade-off that needs to be made.

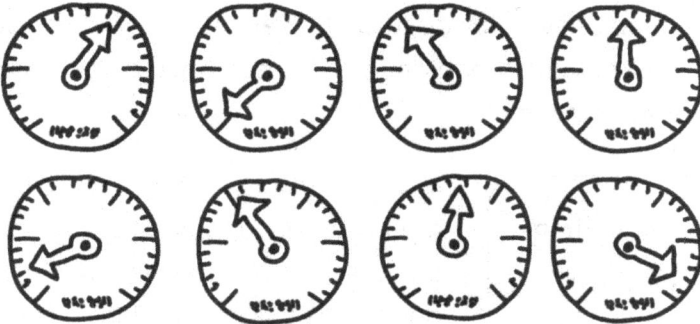

WHICH KEY PERFORMANCE INDICATOR IS CRITICAL?

By having too many KPIs in your organisation, you end up sucking the oxygen out of your execution and putting handcuffs on what your team does, and indeed, how they do it. What more could you do today if you were not held back, tied up, or hemmed in by a wall of KPIs?

For a moment, let's consider a situation which is totally opposite to how most organisations work in how they manage activities and relationships. We will look at a scenario where there is not a single KPI in place, and where matters of great personal importance are managed. We will think again about your personal circle of close friends. These are people whom you have known for years, and you have a deep understanding of and trust. Do you have a comprehensive suite of KPIs that you use to manage your relationship with them and rate what they do? Chances are that you manage your relationship with them purely on their behaviours, and that you have an internal and unwritten set of

KBIs to help remind you about what to expect from them. You probably also give them very prompt and direct feedback on their behaviours and when they are behaving as desired (or not). How many times have you discussed what 'stupid or ridiculous' thing that one of your friends has done, but how you all rallied around to support them?

> In our working lives, we don't have the luxury of appointing or choosing our colleagues in the way we choose our closest friends.

In our working lives, we don't have the luxury of appointing or choosing our colleagues in the way we choose our closest friends. We find ourselves working in an eclectic mix of previous hires, probably by a succession of previous line managers. We are given a job description and some deliverables, and off we go. KPIs become one of the tools used to align this random group of people on a specifically chosen outcome and to try to achieve something together.

When things go off the rails, one of our first instincts can often be to put in more constraints and guardrails to stop it from happening again. Some of the metrics may start to contradict each other (even deliberately competing with each other), and they will usually narrow the possible actions by the team so severely that they end up just following the process, even when everyone knows it is wrong. Even worse, some metrics are born from a toxic position of "making someone or something important." For example, a newly appointed 'Head of Widgets' notices that other 'Head of' managers have a KPI to justify their need for resources, budget, or support. Our new

....

'Head of Widgets' creates a KPI linked to Widgets that enables them to enter that competition. What a disaster this is - an unnecessary KPI ends up putting an unnecessary constraint on people across the organisation so a point can be scored. It happens.

This gloopy mass of metrics bogs down your team and your organisation. Things happen slower, fewer risks are taken, and there are fewer stories of people going 'above and beyond' to achieve a goal. The goals even shift: "Hey - are we chasing top-line sales this month? I thought it was still profit." How can people go above and beyond when they have so many metrics that are preventing them from doing so, let alone 'wanting' to do so? Having such a huge number of metrics gives an equally huge level of distraction for your team, taking vital energy away from what the real KEY metrics actually are.

Proposal.

- Remove most metrics, 'Key' or otherwise.
- Be brutally selective about which metrics are really Key.

I expect this proposal will probably have you feeling a little uncomfortable and adjusting how you are sitting. "Won't that create anarchy? How will we meet the big numbers? This is reckless and dangerous, and it can't possibly work," you may well be thinking?

Maybe. The outcome depends on the mindset and intent of your team. How invested are they, how strong is your Culture? Let's balance our thoughts with two polarised examples.

Example TEAM A: The team has been beaten up for quite some

time over poor performance. Labour turnover is high, employee internal theft is suspected, and the team engagement scores are probably low, but most people don't fill in the surveys anymore, so we are not sure.

Example TEAM B: The team is rewriting what it means to be a high-performing team. They are always positive and seem to be able to turn their hand to anything. It's more like a family fun day in there than a workplace.

Clearly, taking the metrics off TEAM A won't help fix their immediate challenges. There are deeper issues going on, and any changes with metrics will just be white noise for them. By the way, I don't accept that TEAM A is a lost cause. I have seen plenty of examples where a team like this can be managed via KBIs and can turn themselves around. Not always, but definitely more often than not.

But for TEAM B, taking a bunch of constraints off of them is going to be like bolting on a turbo to what is already a great example of what every manager would die for. These guys will fly!

Summary. Team A is no worse off and may possibly improve. Team B will be much improved. If these are the two ends of the spectrum, then logic suggests that everyone in between will benefit in some way from having to work without so many KPIs hanging over them.

Realistically, stripping out most of the company metrics overnight is probably not going to be possible. I accept that. It needs to be done in stages, over time, and with some variation in tactics. Here are some ways that can help you approach this.

1. Introduce the concept that not every metric is a KPI. Start with something like "maybe only 20% of all of our metrics should be Key for us". This starts the conversation and gets people thinking 'hmmm maybe we need to prioritise which KPIs are really key'.

2. Identify and target what the real Key Performance Indicators are. Please do not (and I have seen this happen more than once) go the other way and promote a KPI into being a 'Key KPI' - it sends completely the wrong message and makes even more nonsense out of what should be a simple concept.

3. Remove 'versions' of the metric. These versions can be by timeframe, department, geography, or anything (part of the reason for their growth). They may have been important at some point for something specific that was happening, but not all versions can be useful all the time. Pick the 'one' that gives the most comprehensive insight and dump the rest. Clear as many out as you can.

4. For senior management, only present the KPIs (not all the other metrics). Leave the other metrics as purely operational benchmarks for the teams that run the organisation, or as a way to support and explain why the KPI is what it is. The phrase "What interests my boss fascinates me" will come into play, and teams will gravitate to what contributes to the new reduced set of KPIs rather than the sideshow of the other operational metrics.

5. Ask your teams to identify the metrics that cause the most confusion and add the least value. Listen to their suggestions and determine if those metrics can be cut out, then boldly prune away. Let this pruning become a regular, normal, and acceptable activity.

It does seem that metrics behave organically somehow. They replicate, mutate, and spread like weeds in a garden. And as with a garden, any weeding that is done is not a 'set and forget' activity. Regular weeding is important, and the periodic uprooting should be part of the 'way things are done around here'.

There are two reasons for dwelling on these points and this small but annoying word 'key'. Firstly, it is just good housekeeping. Our curious habit of introducing a new KPI every time we have an initiative or an issue that needs our focus and attention is well ingrained. We can't help ourselves. The negative side of this habit is that we hardly ever go back after the initiative is complete or the issue is resolved and remove the KPI. They just keep adding up, layer upon layer upon layer. This approach is not sustainable. We need to break this cycle.

The second reason is that to genuinely reap the rewards from KBIs, you need this headspace (and page space) to give room for them to become established and valued. Like a new plant in a patch of weeds, KBIs will need space, care, and protection until settled.

KBIs will bring value and positive change, but as it is a new concept, it will feel clunky at first and will take some time to reach its potential. My personal journey with the concept of KBIs started with scepticism and worries. I was firmly in the "we need more metrics - not less, surely?" camp. Please keep an open mind and take this seriously - we definitely have a journey to go on before we can see the destination clearly.

In summary, you need to consider that there is only so much oxygen for metrics in your organisation. Create more space than you need, be ready to support your young KBIs, and keep pulling out the unwanted metrics from the garden.

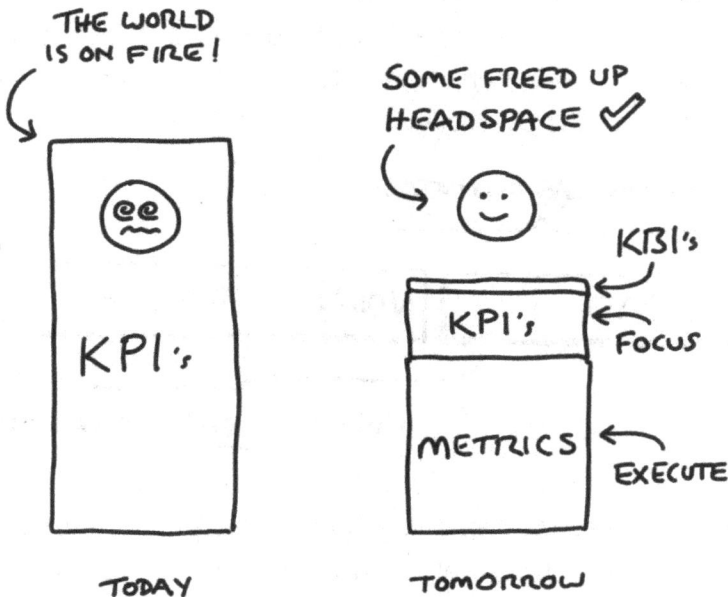

With the diagram above, I am trying to visualise the desired outcome. Today, we have KPIs as far as the eye can see, and we have a to-do list that suggests the 'world is on fire'. As such, we find it difficult to fix the right thing first, and we become exhausted as it seems that no end to the drama is in sight. Tomorrow, we want real KPIs that are genuinely 'Key' and help us manage the big numbers and steer the organisation, we want operational metrics that help us execute the operation day-to-day, and we want a small set of KBIs to help us understand and encourage the organisation's Mindset. There is no magic number or percentage to aim for, but having the ambition to reduce your KPIs by half and then downgrade the majority of them to normal metrics is a good (but confronting) goal. You only need about 10 KBIs, and you can probably remove hundreds of KPIs.

PERFORMANCE. The critical point to understand here is that performance is about what has happened. At best, it could be about the exact present moment, for a split-second, but then it inevitably becomes about the past again.

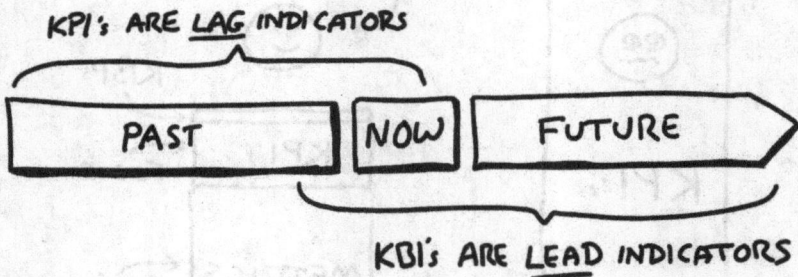

As we mentioned before, understanding the past is undoubtedly important. Using historical information, including performance, to generate forecasts, conduct analysis and research, and guide decision-making to prepare for better future performance is essential. For many organisations, this data is really "a ticket to play" in the way that operations work. However, metrics are only part of the total picture. We not only need to understand where we have been and where we are, but also where we are going.

Can you drive a car by only looking in the rear-view mirror?

Would you buy shares based solely on trading history?

Can you predict a football match based on what happened last time?

Each of these examples contains an element of the unknown, and to varying degrees, an element of chance. KBIs help us build our capability for predicting this 'unknown'. If we can turn the 'unknown' into something 'known' and then focus on managing, and ultimately improving it, then we can develop resilience and confidence that we can overcome anything that happens. There is, of course, a random element that makes some things harder to predict than others, but why not clear away as much of the mystery as we can?

In the first analogy, if you drive a car looking only in the rear-view mirror, 'chance' will govern how long/far you can travel before you crash. Maybe going slower will help you survive longer or with fewer injuries, or maybe hooting wildly on the horn will get some obstacles to move out of your way. But it's only a matter of time before you crash, and the only question is how severe it will be. This wild ride is what it feels like to work in some organisations. "Hey, we can't risk it", "...but we need to slow down". We can't keep going like this." You've seen and heard that before, right? If we instead focus on looking forward and only occasionally check

> As our confidence grows, so does our speed, our distance, and our performance.

what's behind us, we can have a much more sustainable situation. As our confidence grows, so does our speed, our distance, and our performance.

With the second analogy, do you buy shares when the company's share price is trending downwards, thinking that they will bounce back up? Do you have a hunch that they are up to something good or that there is a world event that may increase demand for their product going forward? Or do you buy when the share price is on the way up, thinking that maybe they have still a long way to go, and this is the start of something really big for them? While I can see all the history, what gives me confidence in my decision is based more on where the company is going. History is only a part (the smaller part) of the story. What influences my decision the most is what will happen in the future. Insider dealing is, of course, illegal, but why? Well, because it gives those people who have the knowledge an advantage over those who don't - that's not fair. However, having insight into the mindset of our team and how well they are mentally prepared to deliver for our customers is legal, but it is the same concept, it is insider dealing. So why would we pass up the opportunity to legitimately make the most of this advantage?

For the third analogy, how common is it for us to see a big football club (regardless of the code: FIFA, NFL, NRL, Union - you name it!) that has been doing well but just needs a bit more bench strength to win the trophy? The manager might buy a couple of star players, and all the statistics (and the bookmakers) show that they are now, indeed, the hot favourites to take home the silverware. But more often than not, these expectations are often followed by the team taking a bit of a dip. Maybe the new players don't gel so well with the others. Maybe the tactics don't match the mix of skills anymore. Maybe the stars are more concerned about themselves than the team's result. The new striker needs to score. In this situation, we need to focus on understanding the mindset of the team and how it handles the disruption. If we knew how supportive the team was of each other and how fearful they were about a new star talent taking the limelight (and maybe their shirt), would we bring in the star player? Could we bring someone up from the academy? Someone the team already knows and trusts, perhaps. This level of insight, if it could be measured, could have resulted in clubs spending a lot less money and achieving much better results. Who knows? It's a difficult point to argue, but without the data and facts (e.g., the KBI), how can we prove it either way?

In summary, we don't want to ignore our performance to date, as it helps us plan. It is not however, the only or most useful source of insight about how we will meet the challenges ahead of us, especially when these challenges seem to be becoming bigger, more frequent, less predictable, and with higher consequences.

INDICATOR: This part of the KPI phrase is the least contentious. The only consideration to dwell on here is that the context element is important but often overlooked. Most KPIs tell us what the level of something is, but the question is whether we really need to know or if it is just noise.

Indicators should be like warning lights on the car's dashboard that signal us about a problem. There is a mass of data constantly flowing through a modern car's management system, almost all of this information is kept hidden from the driver. The reason for this is that it is far safer for the driver to concentrate on steering the car rather than analysing the relative levels of the data points available. The car dashboard will display a simple icon in an appropriate colour to indicate a problem. Best practice is to only "indicate" when we need to do something; until then - disappear!

This observation is not levelled at just KPIs, as it is just as relevant to KBIs. When we get around to creating our KBIs, we will need to remember this learning point and balance how and when we should indicate and what a "level" is before it becomes an alert. An additional concept to think about (both with KPI and KBI) is the use of the Red Amber Green (aka RAG) as a way of making indicators easier to assess. Typically, 'Green' means you are within the optimal range where every chance of success is now possible. 'Amber' means you are starting to allow excess risk into achieving success, some action is required to nudge the indicator back towards 'Green'. 'Amber' can also mean that a plan is in place and the movement back towards 'Green' is underway. 'Amber' needs some attention to prevent it from going to 'Red'. 'Red' means you are causing a negative impact and / or that there is no current plan to bring it back under control. 'Red' needs a lot of focus, possibly even a 'war room' situation with very frequent short, sharp checkpoints with senior managers to ensure collaboration, alignment, and commitment to resolving the issues. Occasionally I have seen 'Blue' as an additional colour to use. 'Blue' is used to highlight over-performance, a state of "it seems too good to be true - what are we missing". 'Blue' can be useful to monitor performance to get an early heads up on things like 'burn-out' which can then trigger a 'Red' situation. I would suggest starting with RAG for all metrics, and then adding in Blue to the few metrics that seem to be repeat offenders of over-performance.

In summary

KPIs are good for understanding things like...

- What happened yesterday, last week, last month, last year
- Quantitative measures, e.g. operational efficiency, fiscal
- Helping us plan based on what happened last time

KPIs are not so good for understanding things like...

- How well we will perform in the future
- Qualitative measures, e.g. team engagement, sentiment
- How resilient we are

This chapter is one of the more challenging parts of this book. If you search for a "list of human behaviours" on your search engine, you will understand why. It appears that there is no definitive list. There are some lists of human characteristics, attitudes, psychological constructs, and so on. However, these lists do not seem comprehensive and are more the result of a specific piece of analysis or study than a full and balanced framework or catalogue of human behaviours. I will make a bold prediction that "any codification of human behaviours will be wrong, but it could be useful." I intend that the list of 'things' we end up with as your KBIs will work for you and will prove useful. I say 'things' because I'm sure you will find someone in your organisation who will argue that your KBIs are not all behaviours, or what they perceive as a behaviour. Part of the reason for this is that we will all have slightly different views and emphases on what a behaviour is and is not. Please be prepared for this challenge, acknowledging that the list you create may not be entirely correct, complete, or the best - but it should be useful. These challenges from others' perspectives will be valid and should be worked through with sensible compromises found. Until there is a definitive and broadly accepted framework, let's work with what is useful, simple, constructive, and, most importantly, one that we can all agree on.

Let's start by discussing examples of what is not a behaviour. Clearing away some of these distractions should help us focus on what remains.

Staff Engagement	is not a behaviour	- it is an outcome.
Diversity	is not a behaviour	- it is an ambition.
Courage	is not a behaviour	- it is a characteristic.
Negativity	is not a behaviour	- it is an attitude.

| I'm stuck! | is not a behaviour | - it is a belief. |
| Kindness | is not a behaviour | - it is a value. |

Some of the statements above are more relatable and acceptable than others. There is clearly an overlap with many of these types of descriptions that can be used to depict the human condition. Some of them may, indeed, be unhelpful. In the absence of definitive lists for all of these categories to describe human actions, we have to deal with a lot of ambiguity. Later, we will discuss a simple and helpful formula to define behaviours so that we can measure them and remove some of this ambiguity.

Here are some examples of the behaviours that we could look for.

Believe a promise; is a behaviour that leads to **trust**

Treat people with fairness; is a behaviour that leads to **respect**

Asks questions; is a behaviour that leads to **understanding**

We are entering a bit of a minefield here, and it is very easy to get confused about what is and what is not a behaviour. Here are some standard 'google' definitions to help us understand the linkages and interplay. Note how 'behaviour' crops up a lot - hence the confusion.

Trait: A trait is a relatively stable characteristic of an individual that represents a consistent pattern of **behaviour**, thought, or emotion over time and across different situations. Examples of traits include extraversion, conscientiousness, and neuroticism.

Characteristic: A characteristic is a feature or quality that is typical of a person or thing. It may refer to physical attributes or **behavioural** tendencies. For example, being tall, having curly hair, being punctual, or having a good sense of humour can be considered characteristics.

Personality: Personality refers to a set of enduring traits, characteristics, and patterns of thoughts, feelings, and **behaviours** that define an individual's unique way of relating to the world. Personality is relatively stable over time and across different situations, and it influences how people perceive, interpret, and respond to their environment.

Attitude: Attitude refers to an individual's positive or negative evaluation of a particular object, person, or situation. Attitudes can influence **behaviour** and are often shaped by beliefs, values, and past experiences.

Belief: A belief is a conviction or acceptance that something is true or real, often without proof or evidence. Beliefs can be influenced by personal experience, culture, religion, and other factors, and they can shape an individual's attitudes, **behaviours**, and perceptions of the world.

Values: Values refer to the principles or standards that an individual or society considers important or desirable. Values guide **behaviour** and decision-making and are often deeply ingrained and enduring. Examples of values include honesty, integrity, loyalty, respect, and fairness.

Principles: Principles are general guidelines or rules that individuals or societies follow to guide their **behaviour** and decision-making. Principles are often based on fundamental truths or values, and they are used to guide ethical and moral behaviour. Examples of principles include honesty, integrity, justice, and respect for human rights.

Morals: Morals refer to the specific values, beliefs, and **behaviours** that an individual or society considers right or wrong. Morals are often based on cultural, religious, or personal beliefs, and they are used to guide ethical and moral behaviour. Examples of morals include not lying, not stealing, and treating others with kindness and respect.

Behaviour: Lastly, a behaviour is the action or reaction of an individual in response to a particular situation or stimuli. Behaviour can be intentional or unintentional and can be influenced by various factors such as personality, attitudes, beliefs, and social norms.

You can see from the highlights above how interwoven behaviours are throughout all of the other terms. Measuring everything from the above lists would be quite a challenge, which is why measuring KBIs gives us such valuable insight from across all of them with such a light touch. By measuring behaviours via KBIs, we are crossing over all of these types of categorisations and definitions. It is easier to observe and become objective about a KBI.

If we look at behaviours further, we discover that we can put them into categories. Even though categorisation of behaviours seems tricky to get our hands on, a category of "habitual behaviours" stands out and is understandable. We will come back to it throughout this book. This category is important because we ideally need our KBIs to be linked to behaviours that are often repeated and, therefore, commonplace in the workplace. Habits are perfect for this. As we know, habits harden over time and are difficult to change. This is both good and bad news. The bad news is that because they are hard to change, it will take both time and consistent effort for us to influence them. The good news is exactly the same point - once they have been influenced, they will be dependable and stubborn, especially if they are widespread across the organisation. The task ahead of us is to determine the most important behaviours to us, detect their occurrence and encourage actions that align with them and discourage actions that do not. Then we will see behaviours shift. Over time, these behaviours will generate their own gravity and pull in more people and be demonstrated (and observed) more often. They will become embedded and will eventually become more automatic and natural. **All habits are behaviours, but not all behaviours are habits.** This area is ideal for us to be working on to set up our teams and our organisation for success.

There is a lot of interest and energy in the area of habits and for a good reason. We are, after all, creatures of habit. Some very successful books have already been published on this topic, such as:

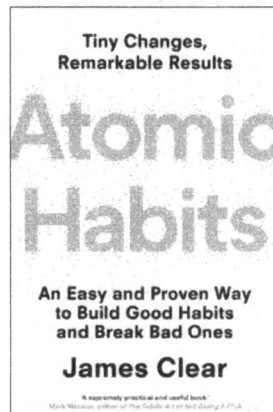

> The change management needed to bring KBIs to life in an organisation can only be helped by a deeper understanding of habits and the tactics that people find useful in making them stick.

What we aim to do in this book is to leverage this thinking and operationalise it so that we can make it a part of our everyday lives through KBIs. I urge you to read both books. 'The Power of Habit' provides great insight into understanding how and why habits are formed, and the mechanics of the 'trigger-routine-reward' loop are very useful and practical for us. 'Atomic Habits' provides perfect examples of where tiny interventions and changes can set off a domino effect and can lead to the wholesale re-engineering of even the most hard-baked of habits.

The change management needed to bring KBIs to life in an organisation can only be helped by a deeper understanding of habits and the tactics that people find useful in making them stick.

Let us go back to the simple description that we used in the introduction to help lock this in and break it down.

A behaviour is
"a detectable human action
in reaction to a trigger."

Detectable - To be honest, my original definition of a behaviour used the word 'observable' rather than 'detectable'. Observable is more than just visual, but even so, it does seem to constrain our thinking to purely focus on what is 'seen'. For this reason, I opted to use 'detectable' to help expand our remit a little. So, for us, detectable means that other humans can either see or hear it. We, of course, have other senses, but sight and sound are the two on which we will focus. We don't want to explain ourselves to HR for using smell, taste, and touch!

Action - Any physical movement or activity, such as facial expression, gesticulation, or posture adjustment. Remember that body language makes up the bulk of the message when humans are trying to communicate. We complete the understanding with any audible actions, such as spoken words, but even sighs, snorts, or altered breathing can convey powerful meaning. While on this point, one of the things that becomes a bit of a barrier for us is the "online meeting." It presents us with a challenge where many people on the call may have their camera and microphone turned off. Maybe this is OK, but just consider that the rest of the people on the call (you included) are missing out on a huge chunk of communication by not seeing or hearing how the person is reacting to the inputs. If the meeting is important enough for someone to attend, then it should be essential to understand how they feel about the content of the meeting.

There are other human actions that we need to keep out of our thinking when thinking about KBIs, for example,

- Reflexes: Automatic and innate behaviours, such as blinking from a bright light.

- Instincts: Also innate and genetic behaviours such as putting your hands out when you fall.
- Involuntary: Behaviours without conscious control, such as heartbeats.

There is of course more, but I think you will start to see what we are looking to focus on here: the conscious actions that someone exhibits when they are faced with some sort of stimulus. We won't delve into how or why they breathe or why some people may prefer to wear a business shirt rather than a t-shirt.

Reaction - This important component of the description singles out the link to the trigger. Actions that may happen but are not connected to the trigger are of low to zero relevance to us. There may, of course, be some linkage, but we will keep it simple and discount them for now. Later, as you become experienced and skilled, you can start to expand your awareness to the wider environment during your observations.

Trigger - We described a trigger as any external stimulus - anything that the human being observed can detect. So, this will include anything from any of the person's five senses. There are also cognitive triggers, which are a bit of a grey area for us here. We cannot always see the signs of the wheels that are turning in the mind of the person being observed. Be careful with this type of trigger. As an explainable example, it could be that the person being observed sees a child that is about to fall off a chair. Not everyone in the room can see the same thing, but they can see a facial change in the person being observed just before they reach over and stop the child from falling off the chair. You may have seen the mental wheels turning (shock, then concern, then concentration), but you don't know what caused it. Sometimes it is worth doing a little investigation to understand what the trigger may have been. A less explainable example is that the person being observed suddenly remembers that they are late for their next meeting. Their behaviour will change, but the detectable clues that caused it may not be there. So, understanding every trigger can sometimes be impossible. You don't need to be Sherlock Holmes and be watertight on your deductions. It is best to accept that you can't connect every detectable action back to a trigger, and that's OK. There should be more than enough to work with that is clear, simple, and useful.

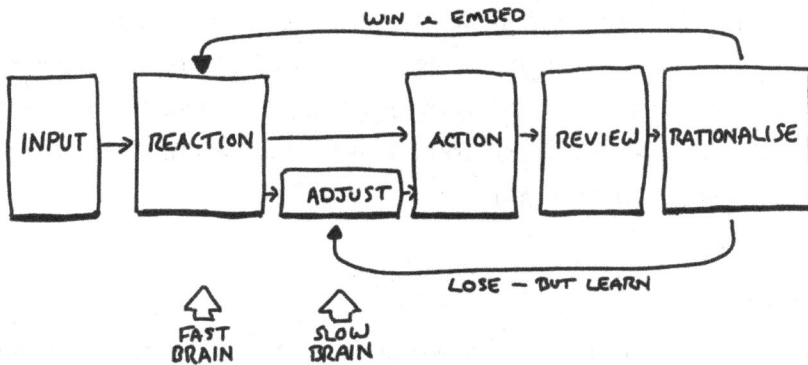

We will now explore the sequence (see diagram above) that our minds go through to process and act upon these triggers. The illustration above shows a very simplistic flow of this process, and we will move from left to right.

INPUT

Initially, there is some sort of stimulus that a person detects. Something has changed, and this change was detected by one of our five senses (see, hear, smell, touch, taste) or came from a cognitive trigger such as our memory of something (e.g., I need to go to a meeting at 10 am). You could argue that any cognitive trigger is the result of a sensory trigger (e.g., I saw my diary or my watch), but it is inconsequential for our thinking here. However, or wherever the trigger comes from, it is still a trigger.

REACTION

Our brain has two systems that deal with this trigger. The first is our 'fast' brain, which includes our genetic behaviours (such as fight or flight) and our learned and embedded behaviours. Our immediate 'fast' reaction from this system may or may not be visible. In the case of 'fight or flight', it should be very noticeable. In the case of less crucial triggers (e.g., the smell of warm bread), it may just cause a memory to come into focus (e.g., the anticipation of eating warm fresh bread).

ADJUST

The second system is our 'slow' brain. It has a limited working capacity and consumes a lot of energy. Our fast brain needs to determine if the trigger means it needs to put this onto the slow brain's to-do list or not. If it does, then we start to bring other information to bear on the trigger to see what we need to do with it. If something is relevant, then we make the decision to adjust our initial impulsive reaction from the fast brain to result in a different deliberate action. In the example of 'fight or flight', we may now be thinking about how best to fight or where best to run. In the example of warm bread, we will now be making decisions based on whether we should buy the bread or change our menu for lunch, etc. In the case that someone might have said something that has annoyed us, maybe we get a chance to catch it and settle on a compromised response. In any case, this part of the process is where your reaction to the trigger becomes decisive. From here on in, this is where we want to start recording our understanding of the 'detectable human action in reaction to a trigger'.

ACTION

At this point, we observe the person's obvious and deliberate actions. Sometimes there are two actions, perhaps a moment of irritation, followed by a constructive question to ensure understanding. Even if we noticed an initial moment of irritation, we should focus on the second measured and definitive response. This time is crucial for those observing the event. Nobody is perfect and it is acceptable to show some initial irritation, but if we see a consistently measured and calm response, then this is what people should remember as the outcome. They may still remember the irritation, but the fact that the reaction was overruled sends a strong signal about the expected behaviour of this person. It is this part of the process that we want to assign to the KBI to focus on.

REVIEW

This process may be internally driven, e.g., "How well did I just cope with that?" or external, e.g., "Hey, what do you think?" or "you know what I mean, right?". It works best if feedback is immediate, and we are often advised to give feedback promptly. For us to process and remember the feedback it is easiest for us to attach and link it to what is occupying the slow brain's focus, so it needs to be attached very promptly. Doing it tomorrow will mean the slow brain has to retrieve all of this information, process it again, and then put it back into storage, which is something it would much rather not do and more often than not, it cannot be bothered to do so. The moment will have been lost.

RATIONALISE

The review helps to assess the Action, and if the resulting consensus was that it was 'good,' then it can go back into the archives and help build up the quick reference guide for the 'fast' brain to act on next time. This rationalisation is where practicing the right behaviours will, over time, build up the indexing system and help make this action become second nature and eventually be promoted into the initial response selected by the fast brain. In this case, the slow brain has less to do and consumes less energy, and the fast brain has a clear index of what it should do. This is the perfect outcome.

> When we think about KBIs, what we are aiming for is a handful of descriptions of the reactions that people will have to the types of triggers they will often encounter.

When we think about KBIs, what we are aiming for is a handful of descriptions of the reactions that people will have to the types of triggers they will often encounter.

These descriptions will become the guardrails that keep you and your teams in a common mindset that will generate the culture that you are aiming for. I've mentioned 'handful' a few times now. What I actually mean is: 10. Why 10? Well, 10 can be remembered reasonably easily, and they can justify a level of 'crucial' (remember our promise about the word 'key'). When you start to get up to numbers like 15 or even 50, then which ones are key? What if someone prioritises 4, 22, and 34, but I value 1, 2, and 11? Can we have 13? Of course, you can, but do you really need them all? Likewise, you can cut it down to 5, but do they give you enough coverage? My advice is to target 10, and as you go through your discovery and move this through your organisation, it becomes a real sticking point to have 9 or 11, then make the concession. Agreement is more important than sticking hard and fast to 10.

The graph below (a highly scientific 'Goldilocks' bell curve) visualises what I am trying to say, 10 seems to be the peak of what works, the further you go away from 10, the more challenges seem to crop up.

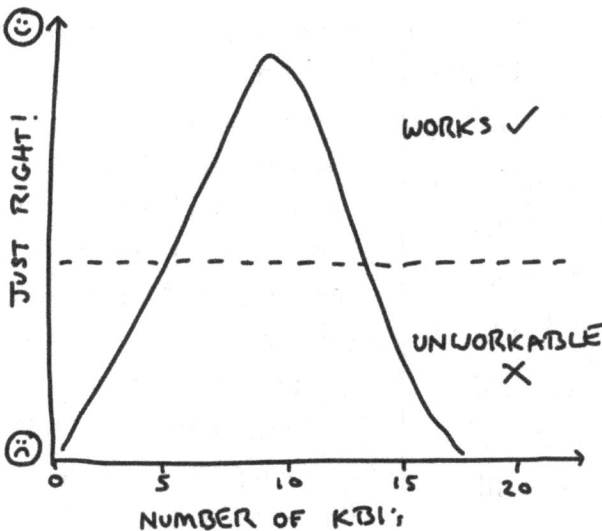

The key to selecting the best 10 is to choose ones that are broad enough to provide good coverage for decision-making (ADJUST) activities but are also specific enough to align with the values and desired culture of the organisation, and then be further linked to the purpose, and ultimately to what the company brand stands for.

For example, it could be counterproductive to select a KBI that led people towards thriftiness when the purpose of the organisation was to make discoveries, break new ground, and invest heavily in research and development. Perhaps actions that represented 'curiosity' or 'challenging established concepts' would be better selections.

Now, onto an exceptionally critical point in this book: how can we capture a behaviour so it can be used as a KBI? Given that we might now be a bit unsure of what is and is not a behaviour, this is a technique to help us gain confidence in doing this. It is a three-step approach. The first step is to delve into what we actually see (or want to see) to clear away distractions and leave us with a clean (but raw) description of the behaviour. Step 2 is where we will then refine and simplify it, and Step 3 is where we will sense-check it. This approach should give us version 1 for the KBI. Don't be afraid to compromise and twist/bend it as you go through each step but be firm in protecting the intent of what it's all about.

> Don't be afraid to compromise and twist/bend it as you go through each step but be firm in protecting the intent of what it's all about.

Let's imagine a scenario where we have witnessed an employee do something amazing that perfectly aligns with the company's purpose and brand. To provide context, let's say that the company stands for quality and produces the most reliable products for consumers. In this scenario, we observed (or would love to see) an employee openly admitting to their supervisor that they made a mistake, which may impact the end quality of the product. The reason why we would value this action is so that the process can be error-proofed and then quality can be more easily assured.

STEP 1: To play out this scenario in detail, we need to break it down. The external stimulus was a mistake, which caused the employee to act by admitting their mistake to their supervisor. The employee did not try to cover up the mistake and instead had the confidence that they would not be penalised for admitting it. On further analysis, it seems like the employee demonstrated a high level of trust in their supervisor, who also responded with a high level of trust in return. Together, they understood that their focus going forward is to prevent similar mistakes. From this, we can distil two important points: "trusting each other" and "being critical of the process and not of the person." This is ideally what we want to see.

STEP 2: Let's see if we can simplify and refine these points into a single snappy KBI description. Our aim is to reduce the number of words as much as possible without losing the essence of the behaviour that we are trying to describe. The following option would work, but I am sure there are others that you can think of too:

"Fixes the process, supports the person."

STEP 3: This is a sense-check step. Firstly, does it pass the 'pub' test? By this, I mean, how would the team on the front line of your organisation feel about this? Is it in plain language, plausible, and tangible for them? My instinct suggests that if a basic level of trust exists, and if the behaviour is consistently demonstrated right from the start, it will be welcomed and accepted. However, if there is a toxic environment on the front line, you may want to simplify it to 'support my teammate' first and work on that until the trust levels increase. Secondly, does this description work when we consider the definition we used earlier to describe what a behaviour is? Does "fixes the process, supports the person" fit into the 'ACTION' part of that definition?

"a detectable human <u>action</u> in reaction to a trigger"

Is it detectable? - yes
Is it an action? - yes
Is it in response to a trigger? - yes

So, how would this newly crowned KBI play out over time? My experience makes me think that the biggest change with this type of KBI will happen at the supervisory and junior management levels. Instead of spending their day on the back of poor performers and hounding them to do better and to stop messing up, they will now need to spend more time listening to their team, understanding the issues, gathering their feedback and discoveries, structuring what has been learned, and then raising up suggestions for improvements to the management layers above. The opportunity for senior management then becomes more about prioritising which changes to make, rather than shouting louder for improvements or pushing potentially damaging or unwanted change through to the front line.

Hopefully, this example will help bring to life how to get from a behaviour to a KBI.

Out of interest, I wonder how many KPIs would need to exist to get us to a similar outcome? This single, simple KBI can be used across the entire organisation, regardless of function, hierarchy, or specialisation, and arguably with much better impact and results than a hundred KPIs would have.

SECTION 6
The Benefits of Using KBIs

We did touch on an overview of the benefits of KBIs and explored some of the limitations of KPIs and why they do not provide us with the complete picture. In this section, we will delve deeper into the power and benefits of KBIs. We will also broaden the conversation beyond change activities and describe where KBIs are as useful in many aspects of work and beyond. It is an obvious but often missed point that people's behaviour stays with them when they go home; it is also how they show up for their family and friends. There is a responsibility here to understand that the KBIs you select and encourage will reach far outside the organisation and the culture and brand you are looking to build.

We now appreciate that KBIs can provide insight that is simply out of the scope of KPIs. Let's return to the quote, "You get what you measure," again for a moment. I am yet to find a CEO or any leader who does not want "a highly engaged and motivated team." If we all want this so badly, why don't we measure it? I understand that there are employee engagement scores, which are a KPI, and as such, they tell me what happened, but they still miss at least half of the picture. They also nearly always miss the point by trying to measure some tangible outcome and never the intent or driving force from inside the person.

> I am yet to find a CEO or any leader who does not want "a highly engaged and motivated team." If we all want this so badly, why don't we measure it?

How can a KBI tell us about a person's mindset and behaviours in this example? From the statement "a highly engaged and motivated team," let's pick just one word that summarises its intent: "Engaged." Now, let's look at three examples of positive and negative reactions to see if someone is engaged or not.

"YES I CAN, WHAT IS IT?"   "NAH - THATS NOT MY JOB"

Notice in this first reaction above; the positive answer is 'yes' without even knowing what it is. This reaction shows someone who is highly engaged. Conversely, look at the negative reaction; it is a complete dismissal. This reaction reveals behaviour that is the complete opposite of being engaged.

"I HAVE SOME SPARE TIME, WHO NEEDS HELP?"   "SORRY, I AM BUSY RIGHT NOW"

In the positive reaction above, we see someone proactively offering up their time without prompting. The negative reaction is one we have all probably been guilty of at some time. This phrase, 'I'm busy right now,' is usually code for 'that's not my priority, it's not my job, I don't care'.

"HOW CAN WE DO THIS BETTER?"   "HEY – DON'T FIX WHAT'S NOT BROKEN!"

Finally, this positive reaction indicates a person who wants to improve things even when they seem to be working fine. This person is clearly willing to go through the pain of change when it's not even necessary. With the last negative reaction, it is the other side of the coin. Even if things are just okay and far from optimal, this person wants to keep turning the handle with as little disruption as possible.

So, if we consistently see reactions from one person that align with the positive reactions, we can be confident that they are engaged and invested in what is going on. They want to help make things better. Conversely, if we consistently see reactions in line with the negative reactions, we can safely determine that they are much less engaged. Because behaviours are persistent, we can now see which of these people are going to be the biggest asset to the organisation going forward. Most organisations have a mix of positive, neutral, and negative people. Can we now imagine the power unleashed if the entire workforce (your current workforce!) started to shift towards this positive state?

To influence this shift with KBIs, we wouldn't need to pick all three 'positive reactions' examples as our KBIs. Our challenge would be to pick one that gives us the strongest, most reliable coverage of what we are aiming for.

> If you think back through all the interactions that you had over the past few days at work, how would things be different if more people (maybe all the people!) offered up their time or resources to help instead of putting up barriers?

A KBI of 'Volunteers to help' could be one that would touch on all three points with a single KBI. Just think about this a little deeper for a moment and how it could impact your organisation. If you think back through all the interactions that you had over the past few days at work, how would things be different if more people (maybe all the people!) offered up their time or resources to help instead of putting up barriers?

Remember the phrase we mentioned earlier: "What interests my boss fascinates me." I am sure you have witnessed it even if you have not heard it. It is a natural concept. If you combine this phenomenon with "you get what you measure," you can start to see the role you have as a leader to both 'do' this and also praise it when you see it from others.

Let's look at some specific examples of where a simple, distinct behaviour led to enormously significant impacts. Some of these were almost by accident and were derived entirely by one person working alone; others were the outcome of a deliberate company-wide campaign.

Customer Service

Supermarkets are not usually known for their exceptional customer service. However, in this example, a subtle action by Emily, a checkout cashier, made her a household name in the neighbourhood around her supermarket. Emily noticed that many of her customers seemed unhappy or miserable. Whether it was due to the queue at the checkouts or not wanting to be doing the grocery shopping, she did not know. Either way, Emily felt compelled to try and lift their spirits. Emily tried to start chatting with the customers, but not all of the customers were interested in talking. Some even seemed annoyed that Emily was trying to chat with them. So, Emily decided to write them a cheerful note instead. During the evenings, Emily would write positive messages on mini post-it notes. Before work the next day, she would fold them up and put them in her waistcoat. As customers came to her checkout, she would drop one of the notes into their shopping bags without them seeing it.

Customers were surprised and touched by the notes and made a point to return to Emily's checkout. It took some time for them to remember which cashier had served them, but eventually, they all figured it out. Even though Emily's queue started to get longer and longer, the people in the queue were in much better spirits. Emily became a bit worried that she might get into trouble. There was a time when Emily stopped writing the notes for a little while. She thought that her customers were in such a good mood, maybe they didn't need cheering up so much anymore. However, the customers began to ask for the notes, and for some, the notes had become the highlight of their day, even if it meant standing in line longer. Emily's queue had become something of a social club, and her customers loved chatting with her and now even each other. Emily's queue was the place to be!

The store supervisor noticed that the queue at Emily's checkout was now often twice as long as at the other checkouts. However, when she tried to persuade some of Emily's customers to join a shorter queue at another checkout or self-checkout, the customers refused and seemed quite happy to stay where they were. The supervisor was curious and inquired why, and that's when she discovered this new approach to customer service invented by Emily.

The last I heard, Emily had stopped writing the notes again, but the queue is as jolly as ever, and it really has brought a group of customers together into their own social group.

What an amazing outcome from a really simple activity. What is the behaviour here? What KBI could we attach to this? Emily's detectable action towards the sad customers was to donate a positive message without making a fuss. Maybe the sentiment we are looking for is something like "every customer is a friend of our company." The KBI could be 'treat customers like friends' or maybe 'treat customers how you would like to be treated.' There needs to be some delicate wordsmithing to make this fit the organisation's language and the local culture, but you should be able to see where we want to end up.

Quality

In the 1990s when Mike Hoseus was the Assistant General Manager in Human Resources of the Toyota Motor Manufacturing Plant in Kentucky, he was sent to work at the Toyota Camry Production Line in.[1] By the way Mike tells the story, it sounds like it was part of an exchange program to enable cross-market knowledge transfer.

When Mike arrived in Japan, the Japanese team inducted him into their part of the organisation by going through extensive information sessions about their purpose, how they valued employee safety and well-being, and why quality was paramount. Mike was then surprised to find himself being trained on a very short part of the production line to 'do' the job, not just wander up and down the entire line and look at it (as he had hoped). Mike discovered that over a few weeks, he was scheduled to learn only 60 seconds worth of process time. They produce Camrys at an incredible rate, but even so, 60 seconds meant he would only get to see a very small part of the story. Regardless, Mike followed the process and instructions but was keen to keep an eye out for all the differences between the US and Japanese ways of working.

One day, as Mike was settling down for his shift of putting a car door onto the car shell, a minor accident occurred. Mike's handheld tool slipped and scratched the fender of the Camry. Mike quickly looked around - nobody saw what had happened, and he was not hurt. Mike didn't want the Japanese to see that he had messed up, so he let the car move on down the line. As the shift went on, his

---

1   I had heard about this story many times, but I was lucky enough to find the source. If you want to hear it, too, you can listen to it via this link: https://www.youtube.com/watch?v=v2mVrdfuVMU.

conscience (possibly as a result of the information session on how important quality was) got the better of him, and he raised a flag. A supervisor came over to see what the problem was. He showed the scratch on the fender, and the production line was stopped. The scratch was immediately tagged, and the car was sent to the repair hospital. If Mike was a little embarrassed before, now he was very embarrassed. The supervisor then spent time with Mike and gave him some advice on how to hold the handheld tool differently so that if the issue happened again, the tool would not slip and scratch the fender.

A couple of shifts went by, and Mike became aware of some other guys on the line talking about him. Mike did not speak Japanese, but he heard the words 'Mike' and 'Scratchy' being mentioned. Mike felt a bit let down that the supervisor had blabbed and talked to all the other people on the line about what he had done.

As he started his next shift, the other workers came to him, started patting him on the back and thanking him. Mike was astounded and confused. "Why are they thanking me? Do they want me to scratch more fenders?" After inquiring with the supervisor, the truth unfolded that the workers were thanking Mike for owning up and admitting to the scratch. It saved the car from failing its Quality Check and, in the end, resulted in saving costs and delivering a perfect car to the customer. Mike ended up feeling empowered by the experience. If anything went wrong again, he would raise the flag immediately. He was now more than willing to champion quality on his part of the production line.

At that moment, Mike understood the difference between the US and Japanese ways of working. There was such a high care factor in the workforce to 'do the right thing' and such high support from the management to fix the issues. As Mike reflected on this, he came to the key learning was that everyone on the production line was, in fact, doing multiple jobs. They were assembling the vehicle, but they were also looking for process improvement and proactively managing product quality.

What would the KBI be in this example? Perhaps 'shares opportunities for improvement'?

Mike was positively impacted by his time on the Japanese production line and ended up improving quality, error rate, and above all – trust at his manufacturing plant in the US. It is a great example of how a single KBI can have such a great impact on a person, a team, and in this case, an entire production plant.

Effectiveness

In this example, set in a modern, large-scale corporation, we will look at a simple policy that saved the organisation thousands of man-hours and created such momentum that a main concern for the senior executive team was how to control improvements rather than how to speed up change.

The policy was called "Effective Meeting Management." Interestingly enough, internally, it was not referred to as a policy but rather as a "core skill" that required a 2-hour training course to obtain. To work in the office, you had to complete a set of these core skill training courses, of which there were about six different subjects. It was like getting stamps in a passport to be able to get into the building and to your desk.

For this particular core skill, the key parts of "Effective Meeting Management" are summarised as follows:

- All meetings will have a published agenda, which will be included in the meeting invitation.

- At the start of the meeting, there will be 5 minutes to openly review the agenda as a group.

- Anyone who cannot contribute to the points on the agenda should leave. Linked to this, anyone who stayed and did not contribute was asked why they stayed. The answer of 'so I can tell my team what happened' was not acceptable as minutes were always published and shared with a wider group than was actually at the meeting.

- Anyone who wants to add points to the agenda may do so, but their additions may be refused depending on time and if the right people are in the meeting.

- The meeting should occur as quickly as possible, and any action points that are determined should be captured on a flip chart as a 'next step' with the person responsible for completing it and when it will be done by.

- Once the agenda had been reviewed, it should be checked and confirmed by everyone in the room that it is complete and appropriate.

- The 'benefits' of having the meeting should be captured on a flip chart (5 minutes). For example, "It was great we managed to finally solve the technical glitch."

- The 'concerns' of having the meeting should also be captured on a flip chart (5 minutes). A 'concern' could be anything that is unresolved, missed, unanswered etc. For example, "We don't know what the sales target is yet."

- The 'concerns' should then be worked up into more next steps (actions) with owners and deadlines.
- The meeting should be closed, and the notes from the meeting should be circulated with the decisions, Next Steps (with accountability and deadline), Benefits, and Concerns.
- Until the next steps are all completed, follow-up meetings should occur to keep the responsible individuals accountable until everything is complete.

Who knew meetings could be so complicated? In reality, this process became very slick and almost invisible, and what would have been an hour-long meeting with sketchy outcomes turned into a punchy 30-minute session with fewer people, razor-sharp contributions, and concrete actions. The number of people in the meetings was reduced to those who were actually going to end up with some actions. The "benefits" part of the agenda revealed unknown insights into why some people were there and what they got from the session. It helped the group understand the viewpoints of others and generated a positive feeling of "winning together." The "concerns" part of the agenda ensured that no one left the room without being heard. If they didn't get what they

> Imagine if you could halve the number of meetings you attended over the course of a week. How much more work could you get done?

needed, it would now be known by everyone in the room, and there would now be someone with an action point to sort it out. It became very rare to hear about a "bad meeting."

Imagine if you could halve the number of meetings you attended over the course of a week. How much more work could you get done? In this organisation, the time freed up by shorter, sharper, and more impactful meetings ended up being used partly to get more done but also to have more meetings. At the time, this was considered a bit of a backfire. In hindsight, though, it was probably a good balance because this organisation developed incredible agility and speed and went from being a struggling 2nd tier operator in the UK to becoming the fourth biggest player globally in less than 10 years.

One of the behaviours that grew out of this format of meetings was to accept what people said to be true. This may sound odd, but I am sure you will recognise that there is a lot of time spent in meetings trying to figure out what the truth was, why we were actually in the room, who has what agenda, and what manipulation was being attempted. What game or subplot was really afoot here? The 'benefits' and 'concerns' sections meant that all this baggage was now placed on the table for all to see. The meetings sped up, and the gamesmanship receded, as did office politics in general.

What could a KBI be to help support and encourage this? Maybe the sentiment we are after is something like 'Speaks the truth'?

For this organisation, they documented a set of Values to help guide their teams in what was a desired attribute from the workforce. One of them was to 'be open and honest,' and another was to 'trust and respect each other.' You can see how these have very tight interplay and how powerful they are.

Everywhere, all at once

Another interesting perspective on KBIs is that they are not tied to a defined activity in the same way that KPIs are. For instance, if we consider the KPI of "orders completed on time", this KPI will tell you about one very specific outcome, and that's it. It won't tell you what happened upstream, downstream, or even surrounding this process, and often looking at one KPI like this one will send you darting off looking for other KPIs to try to figure out why, and then maybe this review is repeated again and again.

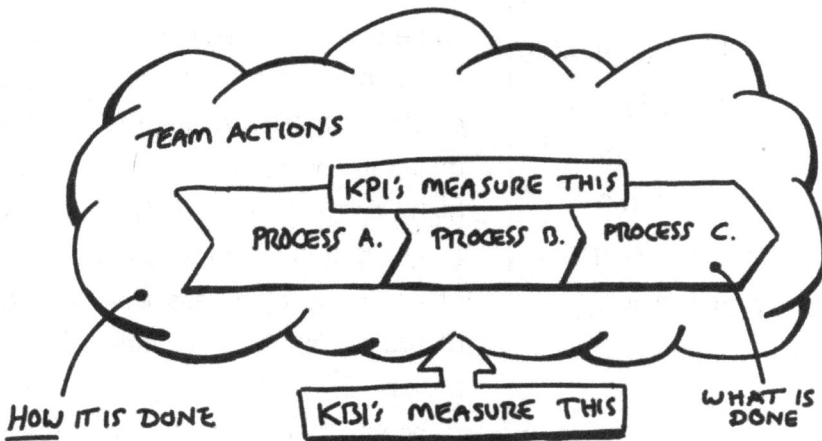

KBIs, on the other hand, are the opposite. They are present wherever people interact in your organisation, whether it's inside or outside of it. Of course, people can act or put on a poker face, but can they maintain this all day in every interaction? People eventually follow the path of least resistance, including how they behave.

One scenario that seems to strip away any ability to act or manage behaviours is in times of high stress or urgency. These situations can often provide the most transparent window into the inner workings of someone's mindset. It is also during these testing times when you need the fewest surprises about how people will behave and the maximum confidence that the challenge will be met and dealt with. As behaviours are consistent, a KBI would give you this insight.

> Business Continuity and Resilience are becoming much higher-profile functions in mature organisations nowadays.

Business Continuity and Resilience are becoming much higher-profile functions in mature organisations nowadays. Most organisations have some sort of 'disaster recovery plan', and some go as far as 'war-gaming' certain scenarios to test if they can maintain business continuity after high-impact events. However, one aspect that is still missed in this type of activity is to assess the mindset of the team. You may have all the bases covered if a hurricane strikes or if there is a fire in the data centre, but does your team have the spirit to help save the day? KBIs can help provide this insight, and they should be part of the assessment after war-gaming or disaster recovery simulations. I have yet to see this done, and I am really looking forward to seeing how well (or not) a KBI serves as a predictor of the team's mindset to come together and pull through during and after a major incident.

Hopefully, from the sections above, you can see how far and wide a simple KBI can reach and the impacts that can mount up. Let's play this forward a little.

Some thoughts specifically for leaders.

What if you define a handful of KBIs that underpin what your brand stands for? What if you lead by example and relentlessly encourage and support these KBIs? What if your workforce becomes influenced and infused with these behaviours?

I would say that you have fulfilled your role as a leader, you have defined, created, and fostered a positive culture, and your workforce respects you for it.

If you ask any great leader, "What makes you such a great leader?" I am super confident that they would not rattle off a list of KPIs. They would not quote their sales conversion ratio, productivity index, or cost of doing business benchmark. What I would predict is that they will call out that they are standing on the shoulders of their team, and that is where the real greatness comes from—the culture, passion, and drive of their team. KBIs give us a transparent way to show our entire team what is expected from them, regardless of level, department, or profession. KBIs help us know how well we are behaving and where we should improve. As we keep saying, "You get what you measure,"—so let's start measuring what we really want. This is your tribe. This is how you treat each other. This is how you win for your customers.

This is not for free. This will take a determined effort on your part.

As a leader, your role will have also changed. You need to dedicate a large chunk of yourself to being a walking, talking embodiment of the KBIs. Don't let up; be relentless in keeping this going. If you drop a KBI, even just once, then you are signalling to all those around you that they can too. KBIs can be tough to create, but they are even tougher to ingrain. This responsibility rests with you and the rest of the other leaders across your organisation. These KBIs and their shaping of the Culture will be your legacy. Long after you move on, the organisation will carry on with the trajectory and momentum that had been built up on your watch.

While I think of succession, another change to consider is when you are looking to recruit. Make sure that part of the candidate evaluation should be on their fit to the KBIs. Are they likely to accept, adopt, and promote the chosen KBIs? Or are they going to be a bull in a china shop and cause havoc for you and the organisation? This is not to say that you need to avoid disruptive people, but 'how' they disrupt should be considered.

Once your organisation starts to move forward with this initiative, and you start to see a firming up of a KBI-guided culture, its identity begins to generate its gravity. This can feel that you are losing control. These impacts may start as drops of rain but will turn into a raging torrent soon enough. The power of an aligned, engaged, and invested workforce is insane. Don't panic. Keep the handful of KBIs that you end up selecting for at least a year, and then review if they need to be refined or possibly consider swapping one or two out for others. Don't do a wholesale change of them.

SECTION 7
Selecting Your KBIs

In this section, we are finally going to get to work. We will bring together the different lines of thinking that we have gone through and focus on our task at hand: What should be our KBIs?

The challenge we face is "How do we filter out the almost infinite (and sometimes indescribable) list of possible human behaviours and narrow it down to just 10 that will shape the desired persona of our teams and form the foundation of our culture?" No small task!

At this point, you have a choice. You can work through these steps now and come up with a set of proposed KBIs that can then be shared with the senior team as a draft to engage them. Alternatively, you can do it after you have gained the senior team's support and have the mandate to proceed with this initiative. Choose the path that is most likely to fit the way your senior team operates. Some executives require a certain level of detail in a proposal before committing, while others prefer to shape the direction right from the start and begin with a blank page.

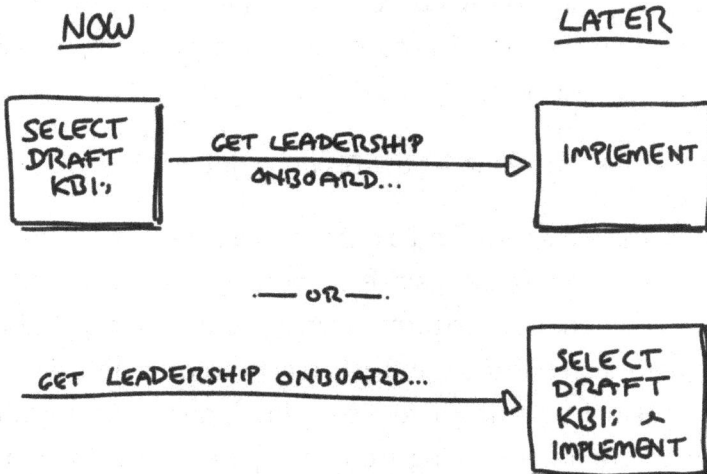

> If the idea of "improving our culture" is already a prioritised theme, then you can go full-throttle and introduce the entire KBI-Culture concept in one go.

Either way, the change management journey will pick up pace at this point. As most change management models suggest, raising awareness or creating a sense of urgency is a good first step when introducing change.

I'm sure you have your own approach to bringing an idea or concept into your organisation. If the idea of "improving our culture" is already a prioritised theme, then you can go full-throttle and introduce the entire KBI-Culture concept in one go. However, if the culture is considered to be 'OK', then you might want to raise awareness in a more subtle manner by discussing KBIs as a way to better understand the workforce, presenting it as an additional concept. As the initiative progresses, the potential impact of this initiative will become evident, and the turning point will soon come into view. The question of "are we committing to this 100% or not?" will inevitably arise.

You cannot develop your set of KBIs on your own.

Our first noticeable step should be to recruit a group of leaders from various parts of the value chain (e.g., sourcing, manufacturing, sales) within your organisation to form a working group. Section 8 contains the full details on this topic and will direct you back here later if you decide to skip this section before securing sponsorship. Regardless, it's fine to continue reading from this point. I also recommend selecting a few individuals from supporting functions (e.g., Finance, HR, Marketing, etc.) to be part of this group. Their involvement will promote functional diversity and signal that everyone in the organisation is part of this initiative; it's not a separate rule for the production line versus the office. If it helps, individuals known for their curiosity and 'outside-the-box' thinking are usually the most valuable contributors to the planned activity.

We will guide you through a process of four workshops with your working group to transition from the extensive list of behaviours to the handful that will form your initial set of draft KBIs.

Certainly, there are other approaches to making this selection. If you have a different method that would be more feasible to adopt in your organisation, feel free to use it—especially if it is already understood and familiar. For me, the following process has proven to be straightforward, effective in addressing change management challenges, and successful in producing reliable KBIs. It's a tried-and-true framework that you can use as-is, build upon, or further refine.

Essentially, each workshop will function as a filter, removing much more than it allows through. Each workshop requires some context and background to explain the activity and define the desired outcomes to the group. The 'why' should be simplified to avoid overwhelming the participants, while still ensuring the intent and rationale are aligned with the cause. An example of the 'why' could be, "We aim to identify the team behaviours that yield the best outcomes for our customers." Mentioning deep psychometric testing of everyone would be both inaccurate and unhelpful. It may sound unusual, but for some individuals, as soon as 'behaviours' are mentioned, they may associate it with their previous psychometric 360-degree feedback report. Reassure them that such reports are unnecessary for this purpose.

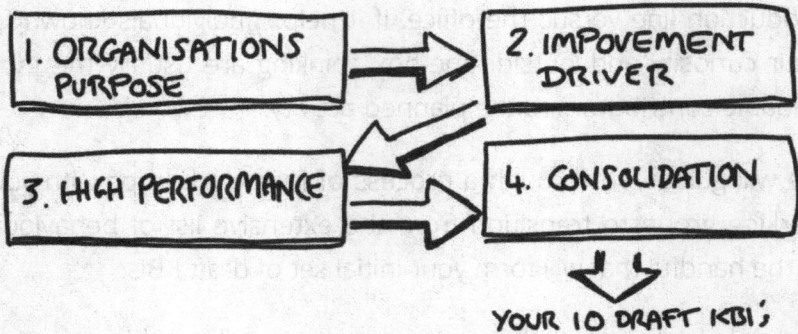

I recommend spacing the workshops about a week apart to allow people time to reflect and discuss the content, but don't leave too much time between them so that the memory fades. While it's possible to condense the sequence of workshops into four days, please manage the group's expectations that this will require a significant degree of stamina. Also, note that if one workshop is missed, catching up will be challenging. Some individuals need time to process the concept of KBIs, and rushing through the workshops might overwhelm them.

Workshop #1 - What is Our Prime Purpose?

This workshop typically lasts for two hours. The first hour involves debating examples from other organisations, and the second hour revolves around determining which example best describes your organisation. "How does this help with behaviours?" you might ask. The purpose of this workshop (and the next one) is to provide a specific framework to which your behaviours can be aligned. Without this framework, there's a risk of ending up with an unmanageable list of 'important' behaviours that aren't in line with your organisation's goals and desired approach.

The task is to ascertain which of the following three aspects is of primary concern for your organisation:

- Operational Excellence
- Customer Intimacy
- Product Leadership

"All three!" you might say. Unfortunately, only one can be chosen. Going through this task can be a revealing experience for many and might even trigger some thought-provoking discussions. To manage this, let's proceed with some examples that you can use to guide the group in answering the question. Feel free to choose three other brands for comparison if you prefer, but try to include one for each of the three possible answers. Don't worry if the group's consensus differs from yours; what matters is engaging in thorough debate to explore all angles.

Apple = Product Leadership. Apple is fixated on design and the final product. They offer you the vision of a secure, flawless, simple, and elegant solution to a problem you didn't know existed. You desire their products, care little about the price, and happily make direct online purchases without any human interaction. While there's a Genius Bar for potential service, it's not their unique selling point. Apple excels in producing elegantly designed products.

Coke = Operational Efficiency. The same formula has been used for decades. They know nothing about you, and you know nothing about them. Numerous other cola variations are available on the market. Here, the emphasis is on producing the product as efficiently and effectively as possible, with a focus on achieving a small margin through high volume. Operational efficiency is Coke's goal.

Google = Customer Intimacy. The primary objective is to gather as much information about you as possible to tailor products and services that may be relevant to your needs. You willingly provide some personal data, believing that it will eventually benefit you. Google's aim is to understand you better than you understand yourself.

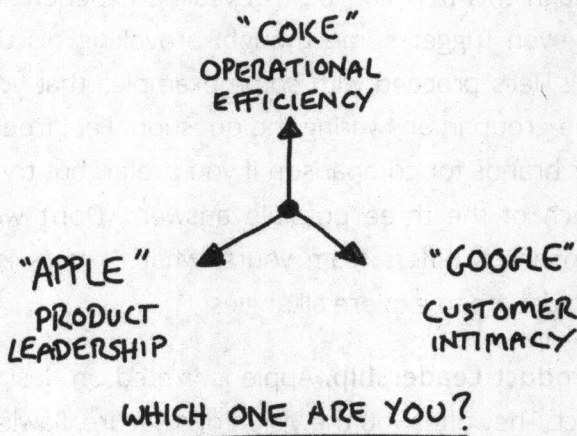

"COKE"
OPERATIONAL
EFFICIENCY

"APPLE"
PRODUCT
LEADERSHIP

"GOOGLE"
CUSTOMER
INTIMACY

WHICH ONE ARE YOU?

All three of these examples possess strong brands and have earned your trust. While these points are common, their Prime Purpose originates from three distinct places. It's worth engaging in a healthy debate on this during your workshop, to whatever extent necessary. You might argue that Google signifies Product Leadership. After all, it aspires to be the best at what it does. But why this pursuit of excellence? Does Google generate its revenue from your use of its search engine, or does it monetise the information it gathers about you to assist its clients in targeting the right customers with suitable advertising? Who pays whom within Google's business model? Encourage your workshop participants to thoroughly discuss all three examples, and perhaps a few more if it enhances the discussion.

Now, it's time to hold up a mirror and critically examine your own organisation. The second hour is dedicated to debating which category your organisation falls under, and why. Allocate 45 minutes for the debate, followed by a vote (1 vote per person) on the type of organisation you are. Allow those with opposing views to challenge the outcome, but you should aim to achieve a clear majority consensus. Be prepared if the workshop extends beyond 3 hours.

> Now, it's time to hold up a mirror and critically examine your own organisation.

Workshop #2 - Prime Improvement Driver.

Once again, a two-hour workshop.

With this second 'filter', we will concentrate on what guides your organisation's decision-making process when it comes to "improvement". This time, there are four options to choose from. You can claim that you value all of these criteria, or perhaps none. As with the previous filter, you need to identify the one that wields the most influence. When faced with a decision to approve a project or an initiative aimed at fixing or enhancing something, which of the following factors would carry the most weight?

When it's crunch time and all other factors are equal, which of the following considerations will tip the balance?

- Better for Customers
- Simpler for Staff
- Cheaper for the Organisation
- Faster for the Market

Alternatively, if your organisation heavily favours 'operational efficiency', you might consider using Time, Cost, and Quality as the categories.

Spend the first hour asking the team to list the projects they have witnessed or participated in over the past 12 months. Then, request them to categorise these projects under each of the four headings: Better, Simpler, Cheaper, and Faster.

Allocate the next 45 minutes to discussing the fairness of the categorisation and whether the distribution of projects aligns with the organisation's purpose and the necessary changes to achieve its objectives. There is no definitive right or wrong answer. The goal is to encourage diverse viewpoints within the group, which will be valuable in the subsequent step.

In the final 15 minutes, conduct a vote to determine which of the four categories appears to hold primary importance for the organisation's future direction. There will always be exceptions and circumstances that lead to changes over time, but a single choice is needed. Ask the group to choose the category that is most frequently accurate and in harmony with the company's purpose and mission statement. This workshop holds significance as it helps shape your KBIs to align with your organisation's preferred drivers for change (how it fulfils its purpose).

Workshop #3 - The Five Dysfunctions of a Team.

With this filter, we will draw upon Patrick Lencioni's insights and his pyramid that illustrates the common barriers to a high-performing team. "The Five Dysfunctions of a Team" is not your typical management book. Patrick, the founder and president of a management consulting firm specialising in team development and organisational health, chose to present his ideas through a fictional story. In essence, the story follows Kathryn Petersen's efforts to establish a healthy environment within the fictional DecisionTech. As the narrative unfolds, she introduces her executives to the Five Dysfunctions of a Team Model, attributing these dysfunctions to the team's struggles.

Graphically represented, the Five Dysfunctions Model takes the form of a five-level pyramid. Similar to any pyramid, the levels are interconnected; Kathryn explains their interdependence, where each dysfunction directly affects the one above it.

In addition to the fictional aspect, Lencioni outlines and summarises his ideas in the theoretical portion of the book. He also offers an assessment tool to gauge a team's susceptibility to these five dysfunctions.

This framework is valuable for us because, as Patrick suggests, until a critical level of trust is established, having challenging conversations (conflict) and achieving shared understanding and alignment (commitment) are challenging. Only with these elements in place can everyone involved collectively work towards the greater good (accountability) and ultimately achieve the desired outcome.

Intentionally aligning our KBIs with each layer of the pyramid aids in achieving comprehensive coverage and balance, with a bias towards building high-performing teams.

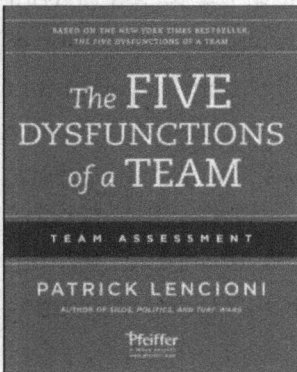

We have the opportunity to introduce some additional bias if we believe there's a need to focus on certain layers more than others. By targeting our KBIs at these common reasons for low performance, we inherently create an environment where high-performing teams can thrive. These areas are likely to have the most significant impact and help us make substantial progress towards achieving the desired Culture, Values, and Purpose. It would be counterproductive to concentrate all of our KBIs on Accountability when we have deficiencies in Trust and Conflict.

Ideally, we should aim to have a couple of KBIs for each level in this pyramid. In cases where certain layers have more significant gaps than others, it's advisable to reinforce the pyramid's foundation by focusing on enhancing coverage of the lower levels.

For most teams, departments, and corporations, the area with the most pressing issues and opportunities lies on the ground floor of the pyramid. I've worked with numerous leaders who sought assistance because they lacked the capstone of the pyramid. "We have everything, but we just can't seem to achieve the desired result." Typically, after tracing through the organisation's value chain, a recurring pattern emerges. A lack of clarity about the organisation's objectives and rationale leads to low levels of team engagement, subsequently affecting trust between teams, leaders, policies, processes, and even the tools required to perform their roles. Due to this, I strongly recommend that KBIs aimed at 'trust' are imperative; it's not worth the risk to be incomplete in this foundational layer of the pyramid.

> For most teams, departments, and corporations, the area with the most pressing issues and opportunities lies on the ground floor of the pyramid.

However, don't go overboard. Even if you identify serious trust issues, not all your KBIs should target this level. You might allocate three KBIs to this foundational level while taking a calculated risk with one at another level. Alternatively, you might formulate such strong KBIs for 'trust' that you can maintain a balanced approach across all levels.

Now, it's time for the next workshop to explore this with your group of leaders. Workshop 3 can be challenging to navigate, as it can be quite confronting for the group to realise that there might be a significant gap at the base of their pyramid. Approaching the activity from an 'outsider's perspective... where do we stand?' angle can help ease the tension.

A productive way to conduct the workshop is to spend the first hour generating examples of positive and negative behaviours or 'attributes' for each layer of the pyramid. Don't worry about the group's initial clumsiness in describing a behaviour as we now think of it. The goal in the first hour is to ingrain this framework in the working memory of the group and establish examples of what constitutes desirable or undesirable attributes.

Here are some examples of 'attributes' to use as starting points for the workshop. Most are positive, but some might be viewed negatively by certain individuals. Allow the team to place these attributes and encourage them to contribute their own thoughts. The more post-it notes, the better.

- Telling the truth
- Being open and transparent
- Being honest
- Demonstrating loyalty
- Trusting others
- Displaying the courage to tackle challenges
- Confidently engaging in constructive conflict

- Upholding our values
- Leading by consistent example
- Maintaining a sense of balance
- Seeking understanding
- Asking questions
- Demonstrating curiosity
- Rejecting complexity
- Striving for simplicity
- Recognising elegance as effective
- Eliminating waste (time, resources, IP, materials, etc.)
- Embracing competitiveness
- Prioritising customers
- Prioritising the team
- Embracing diversity in all forms
- Solving problems without shortcuts
- Self-improvement
- Communicating and collaborating
- Accepting accountability - taking ownership
- Making decisions
- Being authentic and genuine
- Embracing empathy
- Caring for colleagues
- Embracing change as a constant standard

The second hour of the workshop should involve voting and reorganising. Instruct participants to place a single dot (preferably using thick marker pens) on each post-it note to indicate which of these attributes they most frequently observe during meetings, especially cross-functional ones. Once completed, ask the group to step back and review the distribution of behaviours. Then, have them select the attributes they would most like to see displayed more frequently, moving these to the side. This will result in two sets of attributes: one where they are already strong or less significant, and another where improvements are needed. Focus on the latter set of attributes.

> Explain to the team that you will compile this information and share it with them. Then, express gratitude for their contributions and conclude the session.

Explain to the team that you will compile this information and share it with them. Then, express gratitude for their contributions and conclude the session.

You now need to process this information, synthesise, and consolidate the group's output. The goal is to create a list of approximately 20 attributes. These should lean towards the most desired and prevalent behaviours identified. You have some flexibility to combine, split, or refine the behaviours, but ensure you maintain their intended meaning.

Workshop #4 - Bringing it all together

Workshop 4 is where we merge the outcomes of the previous three sessions. The goal of this workshop is to develop 10 clear, straightforward, and comprehensible KBIs that are appropriately balanced across the levels of the pyramid and suited to their purpose.

From the 3rd workshop, you now have 20 behaviours (ideally around 4 from each level) with the highest number of votes (either positive or negative).

Key Action: As a pre-work before the workshop, rephrase each of these 20 behaviours into concise descriptions using the language of your organisation. These descriptions should depict 'observable human actions in response to triggers'. We'll refer to them as KBIs henceforth. This process is intricate and it's worth revisiting it after a few days for refinement. Continue refining it until it appears solid.

Once prepared, gather your group and ask them to go through each KBI, testing its connection to the outcomes of the first two sessions. Ideally, all 20 should make sense, and this step is essentially a balance check. Attempt to facilitate some debate by challenging them and prompting the team to justify the strong links between the KBIs and the Primary Purpose and Improvement Driver.

Let's look at a couple of examples to illustrate the goal.

KBI#1 - 'Asks why'

Prime Purpose: Product Leadership

Prime Improvement Driver: Simpler for Staff

Pyramid Layer: Conflict

KBI #1 'Asks why' makes sense when we want to simplify processes for our staff to create the best product possible. It aligns with the Prime Purpose. For the Improvement Driver, the connection is more relevant to Simpler for Staff than Product Leadership. This also corresponds to the 'conflict' layer in the pyramid. Trust is needed for confidence to 'ask why', challenge responses, and ensure mutual understanding. This leads to commitment. This example is logical, with three ticks and it passes the test; everything is in order.

KBI#2 - 'Has balance'

Prime Purpose: Operational Efficiency

Prime Improvement Driver: Cheaper for Organisation

Pyramid Layer: Trust

KBI#2 is not as straightforward. It requires further exploration to understand why it received a high vote count when it doesn't seem aligned with the Prime Purpose or Prime Improvement Driver. Examine this one more deeply and uncover its underlying cause. It's possible for this KBI to be suitable with adjustments in wording or emphasis to provide context and linkage. Unless refined, it shouldn't make the top 10, and possibly might be removed altogether.

To conclude the workshop, conduct another round of voting to select the 10 KBIs that feel most appropriate and practical. These will become concrete, while the others will be kept as reserves. Explain to the group that starting the KBIs journey requires simplicity and minimal strain. Working on 10 behaviours is much easier than 20.

It's not that all 20 are unimportant, but it's best to begin with 10 and let them establish before introducing more. The selection process might be smoother if some behaviours overlap, but expect a lively and engaging session.

So, there you have it. You now possess a list of 10 draft KBIs, along with others that can be revisited later if necessary.

Congratulations!

SECTION 8
Implementing KBIs

You are already in a great place. In the previous section, you started the change management journey by identifying which KBIs are important to your organisation. In this section, we will walk through a series of events and activities, providing examples of how to launch this initiative. There is a lot to consider, but this phase holds strategic importance that makes it more than worthwhile. After all, we are introducing a turning point in how everyone in the organisation (and I mean every single person - zero exceptions) is expected to behave. Anything less than giving our all to this endeavour would dilute our aim.

Below is an overview of the major steps and their sequence, which has proven useful in previous implementations of this initiative. We will delve into each of them in greater detail in this section.

Sponsor & Endorsement: Locate, engage, and educate the initiative sponsor. Gain buy-in from the entire senior team, incorporating their adjustments, refinements, and guidance. Solidify their commitment.

Select Your KBIs: Refer to the previous section.

The Big (small) Announcement: The C-Suite should come together, united, and initiate the narrative about the initiative's purpose, significance, definition of success, and expectations from every corner of the organisation. This isn't a generic email to the entire company. Extensive initiatives often have limited lifespans in most organisations. It's preferable for this initiative to be seamlessly integrated into everyday actions rather than relying on a grand presentation.

The Strategic Angle: This stage presents the facts and crucial strategic perspectives that underline why sharing these views is so pivotal to the company's trajectory. It lends credibility and rationale to make this initiative both logical and advantageous.

Building the Data Flow: At this point, the rough edges of the KBIs should have been smoothed out. Now it's time to establish the 'how' of capturing data once the initiative is fully operational. This can be one of the more challenging aspects of the entire initiative, and we'll explore several options to construct the data flow.

The Sheep Dip: A phase where everyone becomes part of the initiative. The activities in this segment will take a couple of hours of everyone's time and ensure consistency in messaging, content, and expectations. From this point onward, we have transitioned into the realm of KBIs, with no turning back.

The 'in our team' sessions: Feedback time. Mini workshops for small teams will be conducted, reversing the communication flow. Teams can communicate what they comprehend, what they appreciate about the initiative, their concerns, and most importantly, how they envision incorporating this into their daily lives.

Using the data: Subsequently, we'll delve into how we can utilise new data to evaluate our behaviours and those of our workforce, shedding light on their health.

A KBI in real life: This step immerses us in an operational scenario, illustrating how a team embraced a KBI in their daily work and how life has evolved as a result. A compelling story or example to share.

Rewarding behaviours: This step might seem tangential and is about leadership, encompassing a thought-provoking proposal to take a bold step forward in how personal performance is assessed and rewarded.

To Be, or not To Be?: This step introduces a straightforward technique to keep behaviours at the forefront of everyone's minds without creating a burdensome overhead.

A=B=C: This is a lightweight tool for individuals to employ and remember. It aids in sustaining focus during the early stages of the initiative without hindering productivity.

Storytelling: Sharing and listening to stories that showcase positive outcomes resulting from a focus on behaviours are invaluable. This is challenging to achieve with KPIs, but with KBIs, it feels more natural and aids individuals in internalising reasons for modifying their behaviours.

Now, let's dive in!

Sponsor & Endorsement: As seen in section 3, please don't underestimate how critical it is to obtain the right initiative sponsorship and endorsement. Initiating this effort in a corner of the organisation or within a small team won't generate the momentum required to overcome obstacles. This initiative is 'led from the top'. Ideally, the CEO should be the sponsor and figurehead of this initiative. However, it's more likely that the CEO will need to learn about this concept from someone else. If you're not in the best position to brief the CEO, take the time to identify the person within the organisation who is and collaborate with them to present this concept to the CEO and advocate for it on your behalf.

CEOs contend with various concerns that keep them awake at night.

Matters such as board demands, financial market expectations, share prices, competition, industry developments, and setting ambitious targets with limited resources. Earning a reputation for cultivating a strong culture and being an inspiring and respected leader are also on the list. This initiative directly addresses these concerns and offers a low-cost, low-risk, high-impact approach. Its scope and influence will also alleviate pressure on many other issues that disrupt a good night's sleep for leaders. It could be beneficial to use the flow of this book to introduce KPI reduction, the KBI concept, and the details of how KBIs provide a comprehensive view and ultimately shape and drive the organisation towards a defined and desired culture.

> Explore what factors would drive the launch and sustenance of this initiative in your organisation, and ensure that the proposed approach aligns.

Allow the initiative sponsor some time and flexibility. Explore what factors would drive the launch and sustenance of this initiative in your organisation, and ensure that the proposed approach aligns. Invest time in laying this groundwork; there's no need to rush, as quality time spent here will yield dividends later on. If you have the proposed list of KBIs from Section 7, share them and allow for refinement. Try to avoid adding any more. Could one be removed if another must be added? Share the necessary steps (as per the headings below) and once again, permit them to be adjusted or revised.

A workshop with the senior team (e.g., C-suite) will be essential for the sponsor to lead and relay the briefing about this initiative to their team. Repeat the process of sharing, alignment, and adjustment. The desired outcome is for everyone around the table to stand united and lead this initiative consistently throughout the organisation. Similar to the sponsor, this process may take some time.

Select Your KBIs: If you haven't yet selected your KBIs (as outlined in the previous section), please return there, follow the steps listed, and then return to this point armed with your fresh set of 10 draft KBIs.

The Big (small) Announcement: This step is particularly delicate. The aim is to raise awareness throughout the organisation gently, not to issue a mandate. Past experience tells us that presenting this initiative as a significant transformation with massive effects for everyone can be unhelpful and even counterproductive. A more successful approach for messaging usually revolves around explaining that the senior team is working on their behaviours, enhancing their ability to collaborate, and making better decisions for customers, teams, and the long-term future of the organisation. Encouraging those who interact with the senior team to assist in practicing these behaviours-for example, "let us know when we get this right and when we don't"-signals the importance of this initiative to the leadership. While not obligatory, it is enthusiastically encouraged, even though it may feel challenging. Remember, feedback is crucial and should always be welcomed. Subsequently, each member of the senior team can encourage the same behaviours within their teams and share feedback on their practice.

With the ball now rolling, there will be a temporary overhead for the senior team and their direct reports. After each future meeting or interaction among these groups, suggest taking a few minutes for them to share thoughts on where they did or did not support the KBIs. Encourage questions like 'What did we do well?' and 'What could have been done better?' This approach serves two purposes: firstly, it serves as the ultimate 'pressure test' to validate the appropriateness of the KBIs (or whether further refinement is needed), and secondly, it helps this group of leaders gain experience and confidence with KBIs before cascading them deeper into the organisation.

Typically, at this juncture, middle management within the organisation begins to observe glimpses of behaviours from senior levels and the sharing of feedback. They become intrigued and eager to learn about this initiative, aspiring to be 'in the mix' with the senior team. This generates considerable traction for the initiative.

The Strategic Angle: This activity serves two purposes. Firstly, it demonstrates how using a practical strategic tool can illustrate how behaviours support the organisation's purpose and the value it delivers to customers. Secondly, and somewhat surprisingly, it aims to ensure alignment within the senior team. It's remarkable how many C-suite conversations start with this basic one-page view of the organisation. Going through this exercise helps them get-and stay-on the same page, fostering a unified understanding of how a focus on behaviours and KBIs will contribute to cohesion.

Once the senior team/s complete this step, please don't store it away in the 'confidential strategy' drawer. Sharing it and using it as a communication tool going forward will be incredibly beneficial.

It conveys the origin and significance of this initiative to everyone, indicating that the senior team stands united on this initiative and wholeheartedly believes in it. KBIs reinforce the connection between your organisation's Purpose, Mission, Objectives, and Values. They also build trust across levels and departments within the organisation, making it valuable to share this news and raise awareness through this tool.

Recalling Section 7, where you picked a primary purpose to describe your organisation, let's now delve deeper into this. This approach will help elucidate why your chosen KBIs are suitable for your organisation and how they are essential for success. It also serves as a check to ensure their logical alignment.

The tool we will employ is the Business Model Canvas (see image below). It's a fantastic, straightforward, and exceptionally insightful strategic tool that encapsulates the entire organisation on a single page. For our KBI initiative, we will add four additional boxes:

1. Purpose (describing why we exist and our aspirations)
2. Brand (a one-word descriptor of our notable trait)
3. Values (our enduring principles)
4. Behaviours from our list of KBIs.

If this tool is unfamiliar, don't worry. Someone you know might be familiar with it and can help you understand its concept. If not, there's a book on it. Although comprehensive, the concept is straightforward and easy to grasp. Basic guidelines are provided below.

PURPOSE:				BRAND:		
BEHAVIOURS:				VALUES:		
KEY PARTNERS	KEY ACTIVITIES	VALUE PROPOSITION		CUSTOMER RELATIONSHIPS	CUSTOMER SEGMENTS	
	KEY RESOURCES			CHANNELS		
COSTS:			REVENUE:			

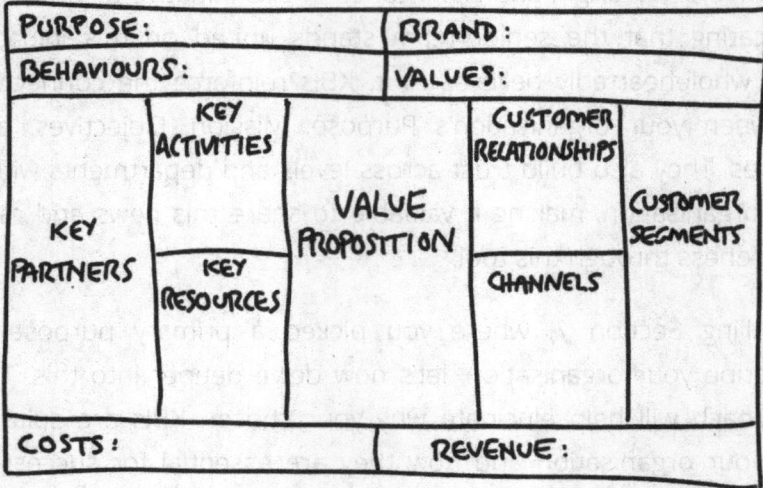

You might be asking, "Why do this now?" This activity might seem a little out of place, but it's usually at this point in the process that the comfort level of the senior teams is increasing, along with the emergence of persistent questions. Engaging in this step now is generally an effective way to tidy up everything and prepare for the full operationalisation and release of your KBIs. Don't be concerned if this step introduces some disruption – it would have been challenging to connect the dots earlier, and if done much later, we would be too far down the track without our shortlist of KBIs. This timing seems to strike a balance, even though it might take you a step back before moving forward again. That's perfectly fine.

It's time for the Senior Team to reconvene and walk through this process to address the remaining questions and piece together the puzzle. Conducting this on a large whiteboard with everyone present in the room seems to work best for most individuals.

- On a large whiteboard, sketch out the boxes of the Business Model Canvas (as shown above) and ask the team to suggest the major elements for each box. The order can be flexible, but it's often effective to start with 'Key Partners' and progress to 'Customer Segments', then address Costs and Revenue, followed by the top 4 boxes. The size of the whiteboard constrains the box dimensions, helping maintain a high-level view and word count limitation. You can't list everything, so prioritising and consolidating the most crucial points with the team's input is a strategic and useful approach. If the team has no prior experience with this, you can find published examples from companies like Netflix, Coke, Microsoft, etc., and share them with the group to provide a reference for what excellence looks like.

- When you reach the VALUE PROPOSITION column in the middle, exercise extreme diligence and rigorously question the actual value creation of the organisation. Be prepared for potential unpopularity. Continue to inquire, "Is this genuinely what our customers are paying us for?" and "Why wouldn't they go directly to our partners for it?" The Value Proposition must align closely with the Prime Purpose work from Section 7. Sometimes, spending a solid 30 minutes on this column alone is quite reasonable, followed by an animated 30-minute coffee break, and then another 30 minutes of intensive deliberation. The effort is entirely worthwhile. Invest a full day if necessary; it won't be time wasted.

- For the PURPOSE (the WHY, the North Star), an elevator-pitch sentence should suffice. The best Purposes articulate a mission that is never fully accomplished. While it's acceptable to describe a future state in an ideal world, exercise caution. Consider what happens when you achieve it – what's next? Describing 'what you do' isn't a purpose. Write about what you would achieve if everything unfolded precisely as desired.

- Include the organisation's VALUES. What primary, enduring beliefs, or principles guide our ethical decision-making? You might wonder, "Aren't there overlaps between these Values and the KBIs?" Well, hopefully, yes! Values are usually expansive and can permeate the entire organisation. A single Value might encompass numerous behaviours. We need Values because they define the core traits and characteristics we aim to embrace. KBIs are more specific but thread their way through the organisation's actions.

- Specify what the BRAND represents. This stage can spark considerable debate and excitement. Challenge the group to settle on just one word that epitomises the brand. It's a challenging task, but many accomplished marketers suggest that when customers see a logo or encounter the organisation's name, they should think of a single word. Strive to find the single word that encapsulates what your organisation stands for.

- Incorporate your KBIs.

- Now, ask the team to step back and connect the dots. Does everything align? Is it optimal? Do any changes need to be made to improve alignment and coherence? Pose questions like "Does it make sense that our Value Proposition is delivered to those Customer Segments through those Relationships?" and "Does this take us closer to our Purpose? Do our KBIs and Values align, support, and enhance the Brand?"

The outcome of this session should instil a sense of assurance that this framework holds water, fostering a renewed understanding and commitment to KBIs. This understanding is rooted in practical experience and a logical strategic planning perspective. Perhaps there's a need for a final adjustment or refinement, perhaps not.

A 'watch-out!' is warranted at this point. Some unexpected consequences might arise, where some elements of the Business Model Canvas may not fit as anticipated or desired. Delving deeper into these areas might be necessary. While we won't delve into these intricacies now, a valuable tip is to explore the literature supporting the Business Model Canvas, as it provides valuable insights into developing each box on the page.

> Some unexpected consequences might arise, where some elements of the Business Model Canvas may not fit as anticipated or desired.

Even in the most disrupted sessions, typically only one or two boxes are misaligned. A couple of focused investigations to rectify these areas and realign them with the rest of the page generally satisfy everyone and invoke a sense of pride in what the page signifies. Regardless of the seniority or experience of the group, this might be the first instance they've seen the entire organisation represented on a single page. Consequently, when you document and share this, the KBIs become a pivotal component of the strategic view of the organisation.

This is excellent news for conveying the KBIs' narrative going forward. You can easily say, "See how they fit in and are integral to our culture and our success?"

Building the data flow:

There's quite a bit of wiggle room here. You have a choice not to capture data on KBIs and not to report on them at all. Sometimes, just the habit of acknowledging how well a meeting has gone in terms of practising the behaviours is enough to keep the momentum. At the other end of the spectrum is the realm of Big Brother, where the team is giving feedback on their colleagues' behaviour frequently and regularly to a centralised reporting engine. The middle ground, or perhaps a little towards the simpler end of the spectrum, is often a good place to start, and then it can be increased/decreased depending on how much more/less would prove most practical and useful.

The key message here loops back to our logic from the very beginning - You get what you measure. My recommendation would be to think about what you want from this initiative, and then measure 'something' that is going to give you that insight. Unless something is visible to everyone, then you won't start the wheels turning, and it will be hard to gain any momentum.

There are several techniques that can be used to capture the data so that KBI reporting can happen. There are pros and cons to each, and typically, a mix is optimal. Here are some examples.

- **Surveys:** Regularly scheduled checkpoints where a random selection of people (or everyone) are asked for feedback on your KBIs. Pros: provides regular pulses of data on KBIs. Cons: may be seen as standoffish and low relevance.

- **Detection through data:** Some actions or activities can leave a digital trace indicating whether a behaviour has been practised or not. For example, if a KBI was 'suggests process improvements', the number of submissions to a "Process Improvement Suggestion Box" email account would be useful. Pros: once set up, this process takes little effort to produce. Cons: may feel disconnected from the team, hard to feed output into people's learnings.

- **Voluntary nominations:** When a team member does something extraordinary that exemplifies a KBI, they can be nominated as a leading example of practising the behaviour. Pros: prompts public acknowledgement and generates positive news stories. Cons: may result in 'you scratch my back, I'll scratch yours' type of KBI trading.

It is worth exploring what other mechanics can be (or maybe already are) best used in your organisation to capture the KBIs.

The sheep dip:

At this juncture, the senior team and their teams should be feeling more at ease and instinctive about observing the behaviours and offering support and recognition across their respective groups. Now is an opportune time to fully roll out our KBIs and allow them to permeate the entire organisation, spanning all levels, departments, and locations.

Initiating a grand broadcast of "Hey - now you can also exhibit good behaviour!" might not yield the enthusiastic response of "Absolutely, let's do it!" that one hopes for.

Rather, let's strive to continue the subtle approach that was initiated when introducing the initiative during 'The Big (small) Announcement'. It could be effective to share some uplifting stories of instances where the senior team demonstrated commendable behaviours and the positive impact it had on decisions or outcomes, underscoring the significance of this endeavour in shaping the desired culture. The time has come to motivate everyone to actively participate and contribute to the initiative.

> Reassure everyone that the initial awkwardness will dissipate, and these practices will soon become part of our daily routines. Invite feedback, listen, reflect, and adjust as necessary.

Allow teams some time to internalise this and start aligning with the senior team's approach. Reassure everyone that the initial awkwardness will dissipate, and these practices will soon become part of our daily routines. Invite feedback, listen, reflect, and adjust as necessary.

Introduce the notion that "we all bear the responsibility of enhancing our behaviours, which is precisely why our KBIs will guide our progress".

The 'in our team' session:

As teams and the wider organisation embrace this initiative, encourage small groups, teams, cross-functional units, and even individuals who frequent the same coffee cart to come together and deliberate on how to foster KBIs adoption within their workgroups. Emphasise that this collective effort will consolidate us as 'one team'. A powerful statement to introduce at this stage is: "The only thing an individual truly controls is their own behaviour." This phrase conveys that unless we manage ourselves, our ability to manage anything else is compromised. Embracing KBIs is the baseline; anything additional is value added (not the reverse). This brings us full circle, as the positive impact of widespread KBI practice inherently catalyses overall improvement.

Over time, as KBIs become more visible, it's prudent to encourage individuals to reflect on where they are excelling with their KBIs and where there's room for improvement. Integrating this into regular team meetings is a valuable practice. It keeps KBIs in focus, reinforces leadership support, and embeds the language of the organisation.

Utilising the data:

Let's take a moment to assess where we stand. We have conceptualised, defined, and fine-tuned our suite of KBIs. We have corroborated that these KBIs align with other crucial strategic tools and are instrumental in advancing our strategic goals. The senior team within our organisation has embraced this concept, internalised it, and is setting a daily example of its application. Most recently, the entire organisation has followed suit, and we've set up mechanisms to gauge results. What an advantageous position we find ourselves in!

The next phase of this process is no less pivotal and will build upon the theme of practising targeted behaviours. Yet, it does harbour potential pitfalls that can yield unintended consequences if we're not cautious. One such pitfall involves "measuring behaviour without causing offence". As should be evident by now, gauging behaviours feels somewhat unnatural within an 'organisational' context, and as we zero in on this initiative, we might initially feel a bit clumsy and awkward. However, this discomfort will dissipate with practice, learning, growth, and a refined ability to focus on and measure our behaviours. In these early stages, however, we're likely to make some errors that, albeit unintentional, can be hurtful.

In the early 2020s, the idea of formally assessing someone's behaviour seems like traversing a minefield. There is (in my personal perspective - justifiably) a great deal of momentum towards advancing organisational maturity in realms such as diversity, equity, inclusion, and the like. Evaluating behaviour delves deep into an individual's core, making it highly personal. As we collect data, refine, update our KBIs, and subsequently make them public, it's imperative that we respect and comprehend this aspect. Approaching this with regard for everyone is essential for the initiative to be seen as a source of positivity, signifying progress. This initiative certainly leans towards a motivational approach rather than an authoritarian one.

For a moment, let's categorise our KBIs into four groups (there are more).

Person-specific: For instance, if Bob nominates and acknowledges

Mary for her inspirational display of a particular behaviour, then this falls under the category of Person-Specific KBI feedback. With this feedback type, it's beneficial for a leader to take time during a group setting to present this nomination, acknowledge the effort, and perhaps even share the story behind it – explaining how it contributes to everyone and underscores the behaviour's value. This might seem evident, but it's remarkable how things can sometimes get disoriented. I've witnessed cases where a list of individuals 'without a nomination' appeared on a KBI report. Talk about snatching defeat from the jaws of victory!

Pulse check: These often arise from scheduled surveys conducted at regular intervals, gauging the sentiment of teams (usually anonymously) in terms of how frequently they encounter positive instances of the behaviours. Once again, if leaders can narrate a story about a team with robust KBI engagement achieving impressive outcomes, that's undeniably positive. However, publishing a leader board of teams ranked top or bottom probably won't work in your favour. These pulse KBI events can serve as a prime opportunity for teams to pause, conduct a quick recap or review session internally, acknowledge achievements, and contemplate ways to strengthen or enhance practices before the next pulse check.

Automated: These entail the digital detection of behaviours (remember the 'process improvement suggestion' email account) and their compilation. However, having automated leader board stats published coldly might only alienate teams that don't rank high. Nonetheless, these types of KBIs are useful for managers seeking factual data to supplement their assessment of their team's (or neighbouring teams') commitment to practising the behaviours.

With such data, initiating conversations with your team about how well they're doing with the behaviours and how you can support their efforts is a constructive approach. Please avoid the temptation to be lazy and hit the 'cc to my team' button.

The optimal kind: The most effective feedback or data isn't necessarily the one that's published. Substantial evidence suggests that feedback is most impactful when it's immediate and transparent. This holds true for Behaviours and KBIs as well. The success of KBIs can be measured by how frequently, naturally, and instinctively conversations and feedback about behaviours occur throughout the organisation. When people start chiming in during a meeting just to acknowledge someone else's demonstration of a KBI, that's an ideal state. Granted, there's a risk of it turning into a game of 'KBI bingo', and it might sometimes come across as excessively cheesy. Nonetheless, as the saying goes, "there's no such thing as bad advertising"! When you witness people going beyond and suggesting things like "in the spirit of wanting to do {insert KBI}, we should consider doing..." – you know you're onto a true success.

Regarding KPIs, the focus typically lies in identifying where a process has failed, pinpointing broken tools, or addressing individual/team skill shortages, and the like. A poor KPI signifies a need for fixing.

With KBIs, a more constructive approach involves accentuating the positives and fostering the growth of promising aspects. Embrace and encourage the green shoots, nurturing them into robust, mature entities. A positive KBI warrants encouragement.

A real-life KBI story:

In this section, we will narrate an operational scenario – a situation commonly encountered in the Supermarket Retail sector. I've observed this scenario unfold in virtually every conceivable manner. It serves as an excellent case study for assessing how a KBI can shape decisions and eventual outcomes.

While reading this story may be beneficial, it's even more crucial for you to identify a story within your own organisation where deliberate behaviour had a significant impact. Even without KBIs in place, there's bound to be an instance where someone achieved something remarkable. Remember that with KBIs, the goal is to raise the bar collectively, not rely on isolated instances of greatness.

Let's set the stage. The scenario is as follows: profit margins in modern retail can be notably slim compared to other industries. Even a slight increase in operating costs can quickly erode these margins and trigger alarm throughout the organisation. One of these costs is termed "Waste." Waste is particularly pronounced in the fresh food sections of supermarkets and, to some extent, is an inherent aspect. Selling the last carrot a minute before closing time is an impossible feat. It's a trade-off between running out before closing (resulting in lost sales and customer dissatisfaction) and having surplus stock, which might be sold or classified as "waste" the following day, and so on. A straightforward concept. The technology available to large modern supermarkets for determining how many carrots should be allocated to specific stores and at what times is truly impressive. Nevertheless, unforeseen events occur, and randomness still prevails. Selling the last carrot just before closing remains elusive.

Hence, the practice of "controlling waste" is indispensable, spanning the retail value chain from the Buying Team that negotiates contracts with product Producers, to the Forecasting Team, Inbound Logistics, Distribution Centre Management, and of course, the Stores themselves. Numerous stakeholders, including members of the C-suite, are invested in waste control, with their performance linked to a set of KPIs that manage it.

Speaking of KPIs, here are a few used to evaluate the effectiveness of the "controlling waste" routine. Each KPI carries a target, and actual performance is measured against these targets daily (or even hourly). Some KPIs intentionally pull in opposing directions, creating a conflict. For example, high Availability is desired to avoid disappointing customers due to stock-outs, while anything related to "Waste" should be low to safeguard profit margins. This controlled tension aims to maintain equilibrium. In reality, all these KPIs impose constraints.

- Waste $
- Waste Volume (quantity)
- Waste as % of Sales
- Waste as % of Volume
- Waste as % of Margin
- Days Stock on Hand
- Rate Of Sale
- Shelf Capacity
- Sell-By Dates

- Best-Before Dates
- In-Store Availability
- On-Shelf Availability
- Aged Stock
- Margin before Waste
- Margin after Waste
- Customer Returns
- Customer Complaints

Now, envision yourself as a 16-year-old student, working part-time (a common practice) in the Fresh Produce section of a Supermarket. Do you have access to any of these KPIs? No, you don't, and that's probably for the best. Even if you did have access, what would you do? Likely quit, I'd imagine. What you might encounter is an occasional visit from your supervisor, asking you to start or stop doing something. However, you remain oblivious to the KPIs and the intricate complexities of these controls. To be candid, your supervisor probably lacks the time and training to decipher all the data as well. Instead, they receive directives from Head Office to relay to you.

Given that your 16-year-old mind is likely not that inclined to contemplate the entire supply chain that culminates in that box of carrots on the shelves, and because some of the tasks assigned to you seem nonsensical (some even resulting in extra work), you opt to concern yourself with doing the bare minimum and heading home on time. You have more immediate concerns than meticulously inspecting the sell-by dates of carrots.

In the meantime, envisage department managers seated in offices, poring over the one or two KPIs they are personally responsible for. Each of these managers is strategizing ways to enhance their KPIs, sometimes at the expense of other KPIs and department managers. Some managers, being more experienced (or cunning), manage to elevate their KPIs, while others may experience a decline. Questions arise, perhaps a task force is formed, or a project is initiated to rectify the situation. Regardless, a substantial amount of managerial time is devoted to attempting to manage all these KPIs, often leading to a whirlwind of activities. Resources across the organisation are consumed by this cycle. Usually, this culminates in an instruction being dispatched from the office to an individual in Operations (be it Stores or Supply Chain) to execute something different.

Now that we've painted a reasonably clear picture of the 'endless battle against waste' from the retailer's standpoint, let's shift our perspective to that of the customer. To the customer, the retailer might appear somewhat perplexing. There are times when an abundance of carrots is available, and occasionally, they're even discounted to be sold before they expire. On other occasions, they're entirely absent. Such fluctuations seem peculiar, considering the retailer's size and modernity. Could it be that the managers are unsure of what they're doing?

Now, let's introduce a solitary KBI into the equation: 'Would I buy it?'

Let's also adhere to the principle mentioned earlier and prune the list of KPIs, eliminating as many as possible. By doing so, we might also eliminate some routines that exist solely to fulfil the KPI requirements.

This KBI is devised to immerse individuals from the retailer into the customer's shoes. It challenges decision-making to be unswayed by department-centric KPIs and encourages adopting a customer-centric perspective. Its relevance shines brightly in the context of waste. As a customer, you wouldn't purchase anything if it were spoiled, expired, or even slightly worse for wear. This KBI is also pertinent to other decisions. For instance, certain products might be stocked by a retailer because the supplier pays for their placement, not because customers are actually demanding them. This single KBI has suddenly injected the 'voice of the customer' into every meeting room and positioned it at the core of decision-making across the retailer.

Instead of an internal tug-of-war among department managers striving to enhance the KPIs they oversee, they can discover common ground and unite under the aligned KBI of 'Would I buy it'.

Another exceptionally powerful impact in this scenario can be found back where we began with our 16-year-old part-timer. A five-minute briefing to explain the concept of "Would I buy it" is a simple guideline and reference point to help our young employee make the right decision about whether the carrot needs to stay on sale or if it needs to go in the bin. It's so much easier than trying to turn them into a whizz analyst and pumping a dozen KPIs into their head for the 55 products they have to replenish on a daily basis.

"Would I buy it" becomes part of the language in the organisation. Everyone is empowered to use it to sense-check decisions that are being made. Asking, "But would I buy it?" becomes a habit and a detectable action in response to a trigger. It's a KBI.

Playing this forward, customers become more trusting in the retailer; they shop at competitors less, shopping patterns become more predictable, replenishment algorithms become more accurate, and the flow of products becomes less erratic. Eventually, after things settle down, waste is reduced. There is no extra labour used, no renegotiation of contracts with suppliers, and no blowout of KPIs up or down the value chain, and customers are happier, leading to increased loyalty.

There is also less conflict between internal department managers, and more energy is spent on doing things better for customers rather than plotting against fellow team members. Employees are clearer on what they should do and are less stressed, trust levels are rising, and employee engagement is starting to increase.

You may think this is a very optimistic picture? This particular example is not fiction; it is real, it happened, and to the best of my knowledge, it is still going strong some 20 years after it was launched.

Rewarding behaviours:

As good as KBIs are, they are not magic, and there are a few things that they cannot solve. There always seem to be a few leaders who exert negativity onto the workforce, whatever the angle is - be it to climb the ladder, gain power, or make up for some deep insecurity - who knows? KBIs are not going to be a

> As good as KBIs are, they are not magic, and there are a few things that they cannot solve.

pivot for these people. There might be a slight deflection for a while, but then they are likely to return to their normal behaviour. A KBI might highlight how out-of-step they are, but it won't be enough for them to want to change themselves.

There is however an opportunity here to gain another benefit from KBIs. With KBIs now becoming part of the language in the organisation, managers can get some support in tackling one of the biggest challenges on managing personal performance. Because the organisation is now comfortable with how important behaviours and KBIs are to the Culture and the way things work around here, they can be used as part of performance management. Surely this has always been the case, a manager can always performance manage someone who behaves badly? Personally - I have rarely seen this. I see people fired for missing targets or not performing 'their objectives', but never for 'bad behaviour'. Instead, these people seem to get rewarded with a redundancy package as its unclear how to get them out otherwise. With KBIs we can add some structure and formality to managing behaviours to support managing overall performance.

The diagram below shows the dilemma. What do we do with people (especially managers/leaders) who deliver their targets but leave a lot to be desired when it comes to their behaviours?

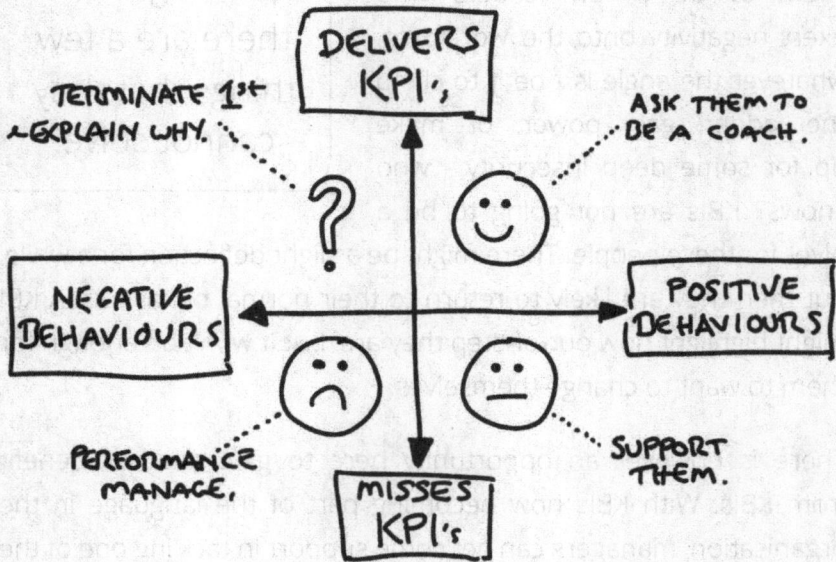

Let's step through the boxes, with the easiest one first, Top-Right. These people are your rock stars; not only do they deliver everything that is asked of them, but they are also role models for your behaviours as well. Celebrate these people, encourage them to coach, mentor, and support people around them, and bring more people up into that top-right box. You want everyone in this box.

Bottom-Right. These people are missing their targets, but their behaviours are still good. These are the people that need something. Maybe they are just new in the role and are finding their feet. Maybe they need some training and support from the people in the top-right box. Maybe it's confidence. You have a duty to find out what it is and to help close that gap for them. They could become some of the most loyal and hardworking team members you will ever have; it's worth investing in them.

Bottom-Left. For these people, the option is unfortunately clear. They neither have the capability nor desire to meet the expectations the organisation has for them. They need to leave the organisation sooner rather than later.

Top-Left. This is the box where we need to make a stand. This person is probably the most dangerous in your organisation. They get the numbers - but at any cost. The positive force that KBIs have on the direction of the organisation can be quickly watered down if this person is seen as successful or even worse, gets promoted. This person needs to be the first to leave. On the diagram, I have added the notation '...and explain why,' which is deliberately provocative and is probably not a viable option in most organisations. What I am trying to provoke here is that if it is an accepted practice to communicate that someone has been fired, then why not say it was for poor behaviours, not poor performance?

Performance Reviews. Another HUGE step that you can take to add some very real incentive towards practising positive behaviours is during the (typically annual) performance review. I am aware of an organisation that uses the following formula to reward employees to great effect.

$$R * B = STIP$$

This stands for Results multiplied by Behaviours equals your STIP (Short-Term Incentive Plan) or Bonus or pay rise. 'B' is a number between 0 and 2. What this means is that if you hit every KPI, but your behaviours have been in the sewer, you get a 0 for your behaviour and, therefore, no bonus. That gets most people's attention. You get nothing! Exceptional behavioural performance is rewarded with a number between 1 and 2, so in theory, it's possible to double your bonus by being the leading light in modelling the desired behaviours. Obviously, this raises questions about fairness and calibration across an organisation, but these questions already exist with however rewards are currently calculated. The key point here is about the powerful message that is being sent to back-up the leadership commitment to practising the behaviours and working on the KBIs.

To-Be, or not To-Be?:

We are all familiar with To-Do lists. Maybe you are a person that lives by them, and your entire life is orchestrated with a multitude of lists that ensure you don't forget a single thing and ensures you sleep at night with a clear conscience. Or maybe we are familiar with them as we seem to be on other people's To-Do lists, and we actively avoid having one of our own! Either way - we know about them.

A simple thing for people to do with their To-Do lists is to categorise them with the handful of KBIs that we have created. This action does two things. Firstly, it helps people remember the KBIs every time they look at their To-Do list. It does not take long for this to become a natural and intuitive thing to do (very powerful!). Secondly, it helps people build the ability to look at a task and approach it from the viewpoint of delivering it while exhibiting a specific behaviour. Over time, this becomes a natural habit.

Let's look at some tasks that might typically appear on a To-Do list of a team leader.

- Update team on meeting with HR.
- Speak to Phil about the complaint from Finance
- Plan next week's roster
- Chase up Daisy on PowerPoint deck for Project-X
- Signoff holiday requests

Now, let's look at a couple of potential KBIs that we may have selected. We can call it our To-Be list.

- Ask more than Tell.
- Fix the Process, Support the Person.

If we combine the two, maybe the updated To-Do list could look like something like this.

- Ask more than Tell:
  ◊ Update team on HR meeting, ask for their feedback
  ◊ Ask Daisy if any help needed with Project-X
  ◊ Ask team to update roster for next week

- Fix the Process, Support the Person:
  ◊ How can we fix process issue in Finance, work with Phil
  ◊ Automate Holiday requests as per company policy

You can see that on some of them, the wording has changed slightly; for example, the action to 'update the team on the meeting with HR' now has an extra element of actively seeking feedback from the team on how they feel about it. The outcome will be that the team will still appreciate learning about what happened at the HR meeting, and now, additionally, will have increased respect (that hopefully builds trust) for the team leader, as they have had a chance to voice their views and be heard.

One of the action points is radically different—perhaps signing off holiday requests did not naturally fit with the two KBIs, so it faced a heavy challenge from the team leader, asking themselves 'why am I wasting time on this - perhaps it could be automated'. A fair question, maybe?

There will, of course, be things on our To-Do lists that do not naturally align with our KBIs, and that's okay, but it's also okay to give them another look to see if there is any real value in completing them at all.

A=B=C:

As with all change, the fewer barriers there are, the easier it will be for the change to stick and be adopted. This tool is super easy for people to remember and really helps reinforce the linkage between "how I behave and the Culture we want". It does so without creating unnecessary routines or formalities that could burden the team.

The detail of the tool is as follows.

Actions = Behaviours = Culture

We try to measure Actions via KPIs; there are billions of possible actions, and therefore, even with a thousand KPIs, we may still feel a bit loose with our grip on what is happening. This is, of course, one of the reasons why KPIs multiply at an alarming rate, and we can easily convince ourselves that we need even more.

> As with all change, the fewer barriers there are, the easier it will be for the change to stick and be adopted.

We sometimes attempt to measure Culture with things like feedback surveys and brand review type activities. If we are honest, we would admit that we often struggle with clearly articulating what our desired Culture is, let alone figuring out how we can constructively measure it.

By measuring a handful of Behaviours (our KBIs), we can improve the measurement of both. We can slim down on the number of KPIs and reduce the constraints on our teams, AND we can provide clarity and structure when describing and measuring our Culture. A=B=C is a neat little tool in helping people remember that what they choose to do (their Action) is seen by others as their Behaviour, which contributes to the organisation's Culture. It really does help people catch themselves and re-think how they want to be seen. Over time, this becomes their instinctive default way of behaving.

Here are a couple of examples of how we can introduce the A=B=C message.

Firstly, as a passive memory jogger by having it on posters in meeting rooms, lobby, lifts, canteens, etc. This is not enough on its own, but it is simple and quick enough to be registered in the minds of the people who see it.

Secondly, as a verbal intro. A really nice way to use it is at the start of meetings, workshops, and briefings. It feels very awkward at first, but it becomes natural after only a few months. Whoever is the 'chair' of the meeting (typically the person who booked it) will usually start the session by laying out what the objective of the meeting is and then go through the agenda. Before they do this, they can thank everyone for attending and say something like "please remember that our actions in this session are our behaviours and they will build our culture". Initially, there will be a few sideways looks between people in the room, and the meeting will then continue. At some point (maybe not in that meeting, but in a subsequent one), someone's behaviours will slip, and rather than letting it go, someone else will step in and say something like "we need to remember our actions are our behaviours, which is our culture". It will sting a bit for the person who let their behaviours slip, but it will create a very strong link in everyone's memory about what is expected in terms of behaviour (and therefore actions). If this feels too confrontational (or cheesy!), then it can be just as effective to have a quick chat with

> Initially, there will be a few sideways looks between people in the room, and the meeting will then continue.

that person after the meeting in a discreet setting. Another way to soften the impact is to say something like "good point, but how can we solve this in line with our KBIs?". This will cause the person to (hopefully) rephrase their point in the context of one of the KBIs.

Story Telling:

When we looked at the 'KBI in real life' earlier in this section, you will remember a point that talked about finding your own story to tell about how behaviours make impacts. This is not a one-off exercise. Storytelling about where people have done something incredible that is aligned with a KBI should be re-communicated again and again to reinforce that the leadership, the management, and your co-workers all really appreciate and recognise these efforts. These stories are as equally important as the story on how you won a major contract or hit a stretch target.

So, we have been through lots of things you need to do to launch this initiative. The diagram overleaf illustrates when these things are best done. We mentioned earlier in the 'Getting Started' section that the cascade of this initiative that starts with the CEO and the senior team, and then flows through to the entire workforce could take between 6 - 18 months (depending on organisation size and complexity). This cascade will start in the 'Sponsor and Engagement' activity and will finish in the 'Sheep Dip' activity and will ultimately define the timeline for this initiative. I won't put a timeframe on each of the Plan or Launch boxes; let the speed of the cascade define them. 'Sustain' activities never stop; there is always work to be done to improve the data sourcing and usage, new employees need to go through the Sheep Dip, and so on.

SHAPE OF THE KBI INTIATIVE.

PLAN	LAUNCH	SUSTAIN
SPONSOR & ENGAGEMENT	BIG (SMALL) ANNOUNCEMENT	BUILD DATA FLOW
SELECTING YOUR KBIs	STRATEGIC ANGLE	SHEEP DIP
		IN-TEAM SESSIONS
		USING DATA
		REWARDING PERFORMANCE

TOOLS		
A=B=C	TO DO LIST	STORYTELLING

The next section has a number of case studies to look at. In quite a few of them there is a small card (usually the size of a credit card so it can be kept in your purse or wallet) that lists out the company purpose and values. Note : This is also a great place to put a reminder that our Actions are our Behaviours which build our Culture.

SECTION 9
Case Studies

....

In this section, we will review a number of different case studies to show you how KBIs have (or definitely have not!) come to life in various organisations. The first three case studies are all linked. They are in the same business sector, with similar challenges, time frames, size, and scope. However, one thing that was VERY different was their approach. One harnessed the power of behaviours, one did not, and the other had a bit of a go but without real intent or conviction.

1. Tesco : UK
2. Dairy Farm International : Hong Kong / Singapore
3. Woolworths : Australia
4. Chorus : New Zealand
5. Netflix : USA
6. Surf Life Saving : Australia
7. The Crusaders : New Zealand
8. Fre'c / C-Two Network: Japan

I am sure that as you read the examples below, you may be able to identify similar situations from organisations you have worked in or are working in now. Sometimes, organisations get very close to the concept of a KBI without actually meaning to. From my experience, being more overt and deliberate about KBIs helps people to play their role and get more from the experience, it is, however, not essential.

Tesco = GOOD

I spent 15 years with Tesco, and my only regret was that I didn't pay enough attention while I was there. I joined in my early 20s and left in my late 30s. It was a time when I should have studied how the leaders behaved, but I was more occupied with fixing the broken things in front of me and being useful.

On reflection, one of the most significant differences I have noticed between life inside vs. outside of Tesco is the way office conversations go. Hopefully, you will recognise what I am getting at here. It's about when the conversation at work gets onto the subject of 'them'. You know, 'those people'. They are the people that are causing you trouble and making your life difficult. They ruin your day, they make you angry, they keep you awake at night wondering about what they are up to, you spend a lot of your time plotting how to deal with them. In Tesco, the 'them' were people outside of the organisation. I don't mean the customers. I mean all the people that didn't want Tesco to succeed, competitors as an example. We truly were 'one team' doing our level best for one person, the customer. In every single other organisation I have worked in since, the 'them' people were people inside the organisation. Just consider the impact of that for a moment. Think of all that time, energy, and resources that are burnt up competing in some way with a colleague. Think also of the negativity that will then creep into every part of the culture. You probably have a gut feeling about how much of someone's day (i.e., your day!) is spent working against an internal force; interestingly, this seems to increase the closer you get to the Head Office. Healthy tension is one thing; institutionalised internal conflict is something very different. It's actually some of the main reasons why people leave their jobs: internal politics, bureaucracy, and micro-management.

The Tesco I joined in 1992 felt sleepy. I sat in a musty office with three other people, where I wrote computer code to try and reduce a process that took a month into something that took a day. I didn't really know why this was important or what the problem would be if I didn't succeed. I enjoyed coding, and I was reasonably self-motivated to make it work. Some people helped me, some people didn't care, and some people wished I was not doing it at all (like the people that spent the month doing the current process). It was just something I did during the day so that I could get paid and do the things I really wanted to do when I left the office for the day. It was pleasant but transactional.

I was there when the pivot happened; it was called Project Future. At the time, it just felt like anything else that was going on somewhere in the organisation. There were a couple of emails about it, my manager said he was going to go on a couple of short info sessions, that was about it. There was no big announcement or kick-off event, not that I went to anyway. But then, a little while afterwards, we noticed that the leaders started acting differently: their language started to shift, their priorities had changed. Some leaders left, some new ones appeared, I started to notice a commonality in what was being talked about, and also how things were being talked about. It turns out this initiative was about securing the organisation for the future. We (Tesco) had the opportunity to be a genuine champion for our customers. To do that, we had to be the best version of us that we could be, so that we could win for our customers. It sounds cheesy, but the leaders backed it up with authenticity; they believed it and they lived it. They had changed, and there was confidence about how they were working. They had set the example, and now they were asking us to do the same. To many, this was a relief. This was not a 'try harder' initiative; this was a 'help us, help you, help customers' initiative. Very refreshing.

Project Future was not a 'dump and run' initiative; it was a continuous drive towards a better Mindset, having better alignment, and getting better execution. I would say it started in 1994 and lasted at least 2 years. You can see from the graph below the impact that this had on the performance of the business in relation to the Market Share metric. For reference, Sir Terry Leahy was the Tesco CEO from 1997 to 2011, and made a massive positive impact on the culture of the organisation. But you can see that the rise was already in motion when Terry became CEO.

Market share of the UK's main supermarkets

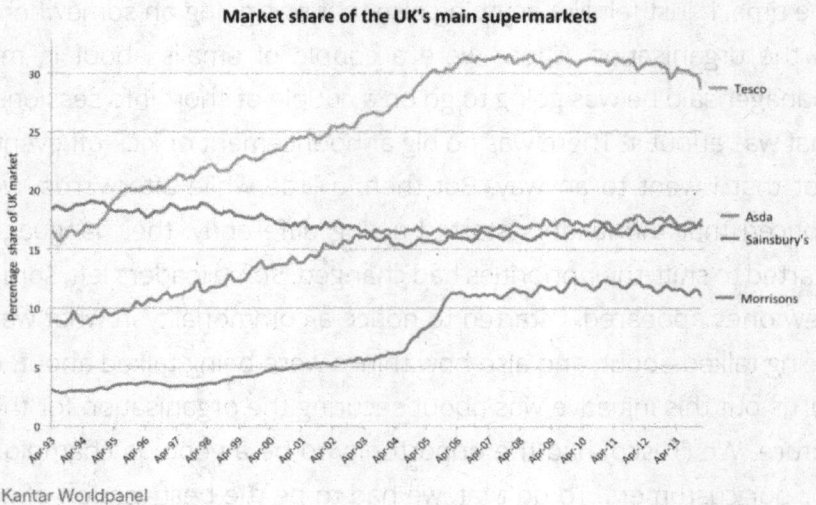

Kantar Worldpanel

Project Future had many components; their impact and power only really became clear to me long after I had left. Some parts were immediately visible, a clear sign that something organised and coordinated was happening. Some parts came later, and I'm not sure if they were in the original design or not, but they all became integral to the overall impact. They built the culture. Project Future was housed in an unused area in an old building; it had been turned into a mass training facility. It was, as you would imagine, an old warehouse, with a concrete floor, no false ceiling, no chairs, dirty skylights, etc. This was not a fancy hi-tech environment. There were display panels dotted around, covered in brown paper and full of simple diagrams and visuals. This space was where we became aware of most of the initial components of Project Future. It was now easy to recognise where the leaders had been; we could start to join the dots and figure out the links between how we saw the leaders behaving and what we saw on these brown papers.

> It was now easy to recognise where the leaders had been; we could start to join the dots and figure out the links between how we saw the leaders behaving and what we saw on these brown papers.

The main components of Project Future were:

- CUSTOMER PROMISE
- VALUES
- PURPOSE
- CORE SKILLS
- T.W.I.S.T
- STEERING WHEEL
- BETTER SIMPLER CHEAPER

Here are some details on each component.

CUSTOMER PROMISE: Tesco publicly made five promises to customers, and it was our job as employees (wherever we worked - stores, supply chain, or the office) to do our best to live up to those promises. It was as simple as that. This made total sense. It never felt like it came from a negative place, e.g., a power play from a new empire-building senior exec. The promise was practical, simple, and full of things that you could relate to. We were customers too, and we wanted the same things. The promises were:

- I get what I want   e.g. the things I want are in stock
- The price is right   e.g. I won't get ripped off
- The aisles are clear   e.g. it's easy to get around the shop.
- I don't queue   e.g. I can get out quickly.
- The staff are great   e.g. the staff are keen/able to help me.

If, as an employee, you couldn't align the work you did with helping to keep at least one of these promises, then it was time for you to go and find something else to do. There was always an opportunity to help somewhere else; movement was encouraged, and the workforce became fluid and flexible. Overworked teams suddenly had a load of extra hands to help them. Stagnant teams with excess capacity shrank or even disappeared. More and more work seemed to be getting done, but we didn't need to hire more people to do it. With this fluidity, people's skillsets, knowledge, and experience increased faster. Knowledge of how things worked end-to-end became something a lot of people had, rather than just a select few.

VALUES: These are ten things under two headings that provided the team with everything they needed to guide their day-to-day decision-making. If you made the best decision you could based on these guidelines, then management had your back and supported you 100%. You had done the right thing, or at the very least, you intended to do the right thing. There was no need to write detailed codified procedures or create policies to govern and enforce all the possible do's and don'ts. As you can see from the image below, it is a bit of a cocktail. Some of them are behaviours like "praise more than criticise" and "ask more than tell," which are the two clearest examples. Some of them are closer to outcomes, such as "trust and respect each other." Some of them are almost mini missions, such as "understand customers better than anyone."

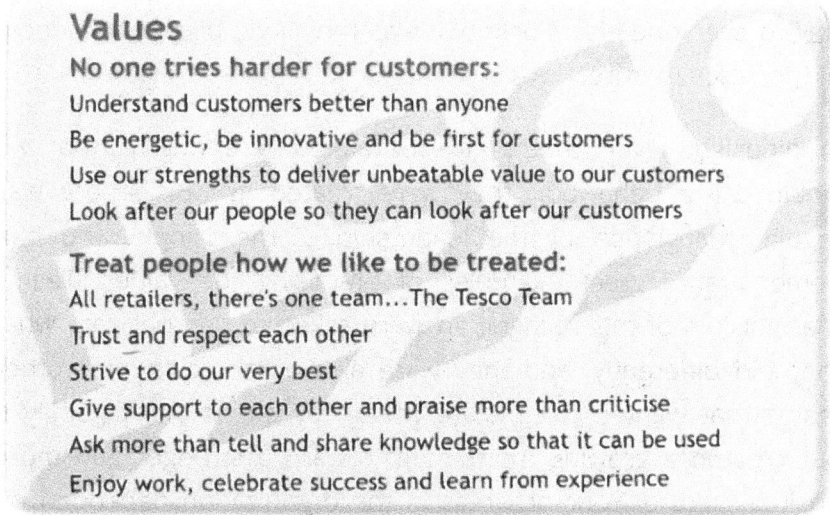

Values

No one tries harder for customers:
Understand customers better than anyone
Be energetic, be innovative and be first for customers
Use our strengths to deliver unbeatable value to our customers
Look after our people so they can look after our customers

Treat people how we like to be treated:
All retailers, there's one team...The Tesco Team
Trust and respect each other
Strive to do our very best
Give support to each other and praise more than criticise
Ask more than tell and share knowledge so that it can be used
Enjoy work, celebrate success and learn from experience

Everyone had one of these cards, and amazingly, most people kept them. These values started to enter the language. They became the justification for actions. For example, if someone started to go off on their own tangent, you would hear someone else say, "Hey, there's one team, the Tesco team." Of course, there were some people who would try to twist these to benefit their personal agenda, but there was more than enough counterbalance to cancel this out.

The two headings became super-influential. Even the sequence of the headings sent a message. First up, 'no one tries harder for customers'. This was not a $ target or an aspirational future state. It was a battle cry, 'right here, right now, make sure you do your very best for customers'. The second heading of 'Treat people how we liked to be treated' was instrumental in building the new Culture. It was so simple and yet so powerful. Think of all the ways that you would like people to treat you over the course of a day; now, make sure that you behave in exactly that same way to everyone else. For me, it was the single biggest influencer of the Tesco Culture.

In hindsight, even though these values were not all that we would call a behaviour, they were treated as KBIs. There was regular recognition by the leadership of the people who had demonstrated great examples of practising the values. Teams that got lots of this recognition were asked to demonstrate what they did differently, and they were also asked to mentor other teams that wanted to emulate what they did. It didn't gamify it but created a growing momentum toward a stronger and more positive culture. Your progress in the organisation depended on how you practised the values, just as much as if you met your objectives or not.

PURPOSE: The Purpose was a simple North Star that would influence all the key decisions. Again, notice that it is not an aspirational future state, for example, 'be the best supermarket'. It was about the present and encouraged the 'right here, right now, do something' thinking. The linkage between the Purpose and the Values (aka the KBIs) was watertight. A phrase that crept into the language that really brought this purpose to life was, "OK, as a customer, am I willing to pay for that?". The word 'pay' did not always mean money, sometimes it meant time, other times it could mean quality. The intent was to challenge if our Value Proposition for the Customer was compelling enough for them to trust us to such an extent that we would earn their lifelong loyalty. That single phrase saved the organisation so much money. It's simple enough. Is this thing, this project, this service, this whatever - so valuable to a customer that they would be prepared to pay for it?

CORE SKILLS: The core skills were a handful of simple fundamental skills that gave everyone in the organisation a standard way to do the simple things that are part of everyday life.

- Effective Meeting Management (we saw this one earlier)
- Problem-Solving Team Building

- Root Cause Analysis
- Rapid Action Teams
- Emotional Cycle of Change
- RACI
- Plan Do Review

> Meeting times shrank, problems got solved quicker, resources appeared/disappeared as needed, accountabilities were crystal clear, and projects were run with minimum overheads but effective controls.

These seven core skills covered most things that office-based people would need to do on any given day. As such, it meant that everyone now had a basic template for working. They were so simple and lightweight that there was no resistance to them at all. They meant that time and energy spent doing something was focused on achieving the outcome rather than figuring out the process for attaining this outcome. Meeting times shrank, problems got solved quicker, resources appeared/disappeared as needed, accountabilities were crystal clear, and projects were run with minimum overheads but effective controls. Change was the new norm, and people loved it. There was no heavy project management methodology or agile evangelists. It was a flexible concept with a simple structure that gave everyone a fundamental framework with complementary tools but also the freedom to make progress without a burden and unnecessary constraints. It was very much 'freedom in a framework' in action. Because everyone had the core skills, you were never surprised when working cross functionally, the way people held meetings in IT was the same as they did in Buying or in Finance. Genius.

T.W.I.S.T: To build and strengthen trust across the organisation, the initiative Tesco Week In Store Together (T.W.I.S.T) was introduced. With T.W.I.S.T., everyone in the organisation, regardless of their role/work, had a chance to serve customers in the store and see the impact that their role/work outside of the store was doing for the customers. It really closed the loop. The week was well structured, you spent a day as a cashier, then a day managing inventory, and so on. This was not a 'watch a cashier' activity, it was a 'be a cashier' activity - it really exposed some home truths! Every time someone went on their annual TWIST, they came back into the office like a hurricane with a list of things that needed to be fixed, NOW! It helped momentum and focus and also reinforced the significance of the Values. Very neat.

STEERING WHEEL: The Steering Wheel was a simple, balanced scorecard. It brought about a massive realignment and apportioning of the KPIs. It also brought about a lot of them going in the bin. The balance was achieved by equally splitting the KPIs that could fit on one page across the four headings Operations, Finance, Customer, and People. This reduction of KPIs brought about multiple benefits for the organisation, and of course, for the customers and the team. It supported the message of how important the team was in the organisation. It had metrics to truly understand if we were living up to the promise to customers and thinned out the distraction from thousands of Operational and Financial KPIs. Managers' performance was appraised on how well they supported the entire Steering Wheel, not just a single KPI on it.

In this updated Steering Wheel, you can see that further balancing happened with the addition of the COMMUNITY segment. You can still see the original customer promise and the two headings for the Values (KBIs). Note how they form the inner ring of the wheel, and how the customer catchphrase is at the centre as a guiding star. Superb alignment.

BETTER, SIMPLER, CHEAPER: A simple mantra that everyone could use when trying to do something different: Is this Better-for-Customers? Is it Simpler-for-Staff? Is it Cheaper-for-Tesco? Three yeses mean get on and do it! Two means "hmm, maybe", let's see if we can improve it. One "no" - back to the drawing board. None, "why are you even asking?".

The outcome was incredible. Imagine if you put a thousand people onto a large playing field, you would have seen them milling around in all different directions, bumping into each other, weaving around, trying to find someone or something. With Project Future, it felt like all people in the organisation started to walk in the same direction without being told which way to go. It was mesmerising to watch such a large number of people change direction and speed as a group. You could just sense the crackle in the atmosphere. Instead of management pointing the way and trying to rally the troops and generate some energy, the biggest challenge now was how to channel it, steer it, and stop it from overheating. Tesco went on to become the customer darling of the UK and ultimately rose further to become the 4th largest retailer in the world.

Without Project Future, the cornerstone for Tesco to build from would not have been placed. Today, almost 30 years after Project Future, it is still possible to detect the echo of this Culture inside Tesco. It is not exactly the same as it was; it has evolved - good. But it is still distinctive, still strong, and still winning for customers. I believe there are two main reasons for it being so embedded and sustainable. Firstly, everything was so clearly and obviously linked. The KBIs (Values), Purpose, Promise, Core Skills, and so on all supported each other. Secondly, the KBIs influenced individual behaviour, which became the behaviours of the organisation, and then by default, defined the winning Culture. When I now bump into ex-Tesco people elsewhere in the world, it is amazing how many of them talk about introducing these ways of working into their new organisations. Why would they do that if it wasn't such a winning formula?

It is a great example of how stubborn and resilient a Culture can be to still be observable 30 years after it came into being.

Dairy Farm International = NOT SO GOOD

I won't spend so long on this example. The story is probably familiar enough and will be easily recognisable because it is, unfortunately, the 'usual' story. In fact, I will only dwell on a single point of comparison. It is the little card that was handed out to employees.

Dairy
Farm

Corporate Mission

To be the Leading Retailer in Asia in terms of Sales and long-term shareholder Value Creation.

Dairy
Farm

3-YEAR STRATEGY PLAN 2011-2013

MAKE IT HAPPEN

1. Drive Group Procurement Participation
2. Drive Corporate Brands
3. Accelerate GMS sales
4. Standardize Business Processes & Systems
5. Address Underperformers
6. Improve Supply Chain Processes
7. Focus on Fresh
8. Extend the Reach of Our Existing Businesses
9. Build Strategic Competence & Retail Brand Equity
10. Develop, Motivate and Nurture Our Talent

Know our customers, meet their needs

Let's begin with the Purpose, or Corporate Mission, as it is noted here. Even that subtle change of heading is enough to set the scene. A Mission suggests we 'do it then go home', whereas a Purpose has more longevity and enduring sustainability. Notice how this example specifies the future state. There is no mention of customers; quite the opposite, the objective is to create value for the shareholders. It is even specific enough to point out that 'sales' is the only important thing in creating that value. It is not inspirational and is already bound by substantial constraints.

Let's look at the flip side of the card. There are definitely no clues on how to behave or conduct yourself. Nothing that you can relate to, such as a Value, a KBI, an attitude, or a belief. It is a stone-cold list of things to 'make it happen', as is pointed out at the top. There is no easy linkage between the list of 10 things and the corporate mission; you need to have faith that the leadership team knows that these 10 things will deliver the mission. The list is, in fact, a list of initiatives rather than a list of things to aspire to.

Think about initiative number 5 for a moment. As an employee in that organisation, how would that make you feel? You probably have little idea why you are there or what it takes to be successful. You are given no guidelines on what it takes to be useful; the only thing you have from this card is the threat that if you don't work it out (i.e. deliver your KPIs, most probably at any cost), you are gone.

I find it quite sad that the concession to customers is at the bottom of the card. It is really a bit of a backhanded threat, 'Know our customers, meet their needs' or else (please see initiative number 5)!

How this played out was extremely demotivating. There was complete apathy across the office; the link between what I did at my desk and what customers wanted from the team in the stores did not exist. In the eyes of many managers, the more complicated it became to 'do' something in the office, the more essential they became to oversee such complexity. What other measure of importance or success did they have? Despite all this, the staff in the stores undertook the daily battle to try and hit an ever-changing, ever-confusing, ever-increasing laundry list of KPIs with ever-dwindling resources and capability. There was only one outcome: KPIs were missed, sales declined, and people left.

I like to think of myself as quite a resilient person, but after less than two years at Dairy Farm, I was one of the people who left. It was clear that no matter what individuals did across the organisation, little progress was going to be made. There was no point in carrying on when the environment was working against everyone. My decision to leave was not because of the rewards, the scope of the role, the people I worked with on a daily basis, or even the fact we were in tough trading conditions. It was primarily due to poor leadership behaviours. Some of my peers left before me, the rest after me; my manager left within the next six months.

Woolworths = GETTING THERE

In this third case study, I will focus on the same single artifact once again: the little card handed out to employees. From the previous two examples, you should now have a keen eye for what is useful from a KBI point of view and what is corporate noise and constraints.

These cards appeared as part of a transformation program; it was likely a deliberate effort to energise the workforce to change. The main ambition of the transformation program was to make savings to enable the organisation to invest in growth.

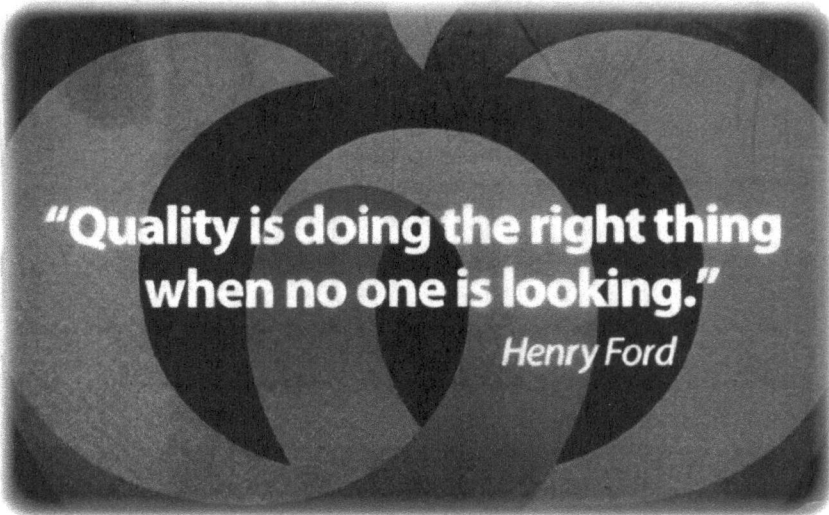

It's interesting that the statement on the front of the card (above) is from someone else, Henry Ford. While thought-provoking, it's not an obvious Purpose or Mission for Woolworths. It's not customer or team-focused, and it simply highlights the insight of someone else. There needs to be an assumption made that Quality is important for Woolworths, but it's a little unclear how, why, or where. Let's assume it's important "everywhere" for the moment.

On the back of the card (below), it's stated that Woolworths' secret sauce is the ability to "control costs and deliver efficiencies." This statement implies that the secret sauce is not the employees. The foundation on which everything is built is about being thrifty and efficient, which contradicts the front of the card, where Quality is emphasised. Prioritising both Quality and Efficiency is challenging as they compete for resources, so it's now becoming confusing.

The boxes across the centre of the card call out some functional corporate components and initiatives. However, as an employee, it leaves you wondering if you're not working on or in any of those things, are you of any value? Should you move to one of those areas to have a chance to progress?

The roof of the house is the highlight of the card. It's something the team can now relate to, and it's something we can attach a KBI to. This narrowing (fresh ways) of the ambition is strange, but the overall sentiment is good.

There is nothing else here on behaviours or cultural aspirations, which is a missed opportunity. The culture in Woolworths was better than in Dairy Farm International but not as strong as in Tesco.

These three examples show that these little cards (or lobby / meeting room posters) are a good indicator of an organisation's thinking around encouraging the right mindset, behaviours, and culture. If your organisation has one of these cards, have a look and see what it is saying. Is it in line with the Purpose, Brand, Behaviours, and Values of your Business Model Canvas? Can you make links to behaviours and culture anywhere?

Chorus New Zealand (written by Adam Bentley)

To tell the Chorus KBI story, I need to transport you back to a simpler time when there was no internet, no cell phones, your telco provider was a government monopoly, and you only had a landline. If you were fancy, you had a fax machine.

Chorus was just a twinkle in a future government's eye then. Back then, NZ Post Office had all the critical infrastructure providers under its broad roof. Over time, all these utilities broke away, reforming to become competitive private entities. The telco sector was no different. Telecom was the first iteration, and when the internet arrived, and it became evident that someone needed to build better connections, Telecom split into Chorus, the infrastructure builder, and Telecom Retail, the service provider.

It was here that the Chorus KBI story began. Eighty people walked out of Telecom House, removed their Telecom ties, and started building a fibre broadband network for New Zealanders under a new private company, Chorus.

The eighty pioneers in that first iteration of Chorus were all network-facing people with solid connections and relationships with industry suppliers. This period post-separation was a time in Chorus when everybody knew everybody else; it felt like a like-minded work family.

The CEO at the time, Mark Ratcliffe, recognised the overwhelmingly large undertaking they were about to embark on. He realised that building something brand new of this scale while establishing a new company would require more than simply managing by KPIs or targets. He started with one simple Key Behavioural Indicator (KBI), 'we care'.

'We care' was not written down or put on colourful posters on the office wall; it lived in all interactions. For example, they cared about their people, the quality of the network, and their relationships with stakeholders. Chorus needed something different to succeed in such a daunting environment, and a KBI provided this.

Fast forward 11 years, Chorus has had new CEOs, built the lion's share of a new fibre network that reaches 87 per cent of the population, and grown to a team of about 800. Yet, it still retains the essence of 'we care'.

Again, you wouldn't know it from any fancy poster or mission statement. The legacy has lived on through actions and embedded culture. The custodians of this culture, the successive CEOs, and executives, all walk the walk and have developed a contemporary, meaningful purpose and values for Chorus that brings 'we care' to life.

Connecting Aotearoa so that we can all live, learn, work and play
CURIOUS
COURAGEOUS
COLLABORATIVE
AUTHENTIC

You can see that Chorus' purpose centres around making Aotearoa New Zealand a better place. The values that hold meaning for Chorus translate into behaviours: curiosity, courage, collaboration, and authenticity. While other aspects of this vision discuss achieving the purpose and value creation, they are not the centrepiece.

So, how does this manifest? And how do you sustain it? Let's start with how it shows up. I will share some personal stories demonstrating how "we care" as a behaviour is evident.

I joined Chorus in March 2021. My induction was initially planned at the Auckland corporate office, about a three-hour drive from where I live. I had driven up to Auckland the night before and stayed with friends. While enjoying dinner with them, our Prime Minister announced that Auckland was about to go into an indefinite lockdown, and anyone living outside of Auckland had until midnight that night to leave. Oh dear, time to go!

As I left the soon-to-be locked-down city, my boss called to apologise that the induction in Auckland wouldn't work out. However, he suggested I go to the Hamilton corporate office the next day instead. I arrived home just before midnight and was on the road again by 6 am, as Hamilton is a two-hour drive away. Upon arriving in Hamilton, I realised that the office had also decided to work from home as a precaution. Oh dear, part two. My boss then said not to worry and that there was a regional office in Tauranga, where I live, and they could at least show me how to log in before figuring out the next steps. So, I drove back.

When I arrived at the Tauranga office, I had been driving for 10 hours out of the last 20! It's safe to say I was exhausted. The colleague who met me at the regional Tauranga office was a senior manager from another business area. He had only received 30 minutes' notice that I was coming and needed help logging in. He went above and beyond. He cancelled all his meetings for the day and provided me with a comprehensive induction and a fantastic overview of the company. He made me feel incredibly welcome and special that day, despite having no obligation to do so. When I thanked him at the end of the day, he was genuinely surprised that I found it noteworthy. He demonstrated care for each other without a moment's hesitation or consideration of any other alternative.

The other story is about my role in closing out recommendations made by an external auditor regarding our injury return-to-work procedures. I brought in a return-to-work specialist consultant who reviewed our policies, delved into our practices, and interviewed numerous team members. She found that there appeared to be universal care for each other but little in documented processes. We needed to balance being overly prescriptive and relying on the team's natural sense of respect.

One example stands out in my mind. The consultant asked me about the process if a team member was injured at work and needed to be taken to a doctor. What was the procedure for the accompanying team member to take time off? Who would pay the doctor's bill? There needed to be documentation for this procedure. I responded that I believed nobody would ever prioritise work over accompanying an injured team member to the doctor, and they would probably pay the bill and get reimbursed later. We never needed a procedure because it was something that would naturally happen.

The consultant rightfully pressed me further, asking how I knew this. I had no ready answer because we have so few incidents. How few? We have a Lost Time Frequency Rate (LTFR) that is half of the industry average.

> This is an excellent example of the ingrained KBI of 'we care' surpassing KPIs or rigid documentation.

As I relayed this to the consultant, she couldn't help but laugh and say, "It's evident that there is a correlation between culture and safety outcomes!" So, we documented the minimum legislated requirements and allowed everyone to proceed with their work. This is an excellent example of the ingrained KBI of 'we care' surpassing KPIs or rigid documentation.

How does Chorus sustain this culture? One notable practice is that there is a deep-rooted culture of valuing mindset over skillset during the hiring process. A final culture fit interview is conducted with a peer team member as part of the recruitment process. It is as simple as grabbing a coffee and having a conversation to determine if the potential recruit would fit into the team.

A wide range of actions supports this culture, including prioritising work aligned with the purpose and measuring success based on balanced scorecard outcomes, including behaviours. Examples of Chorus behaviours that are looked for and encouraged are:

Quality Management

- We care about our customers and the quality of the services they receive.
- We care that our staff know what good looks like and are set up for success.
- We care that risks are identified and reported in the workplace and ensure that we mitigate these.
- We care about honouring our commitments and prioritising actions to close performance gaps.
- We care about making tomorrow's workplace better than yesterday's.

Health & Safety

- We care that our leaders take practicable steps to keep our staff safe.
- We care that potential hazards are called out in the

workplace, and staff know what to do when things go wrong or in the event of an emergency.

- We care that Health and Safety is planned for and has a non-negotiable place in our strategy.
- We care that Health & Safety performance is measured, reviewed, and improved.
- We care that our staff are supported when returning to work after an injury.

In summary, this case study demonstrates that KBIs, when integrated into the organisation, not only endure but become 'just the way we do things around here.'

5. Netflix = FAMOUSLY GREAT!

I will approach this case study (more of an observation to be honest) from a very specific angle. There has been a lot written about the Netflix Culture, almost all of it exceptionally positive. This is extract is no different. Patty McCord was the chief talent officer at Netflix from 1998 to 2012 and now advises start-ups and entrepreneurs. She is the author of Powerful: Building a Culture of Freedom and Responsibility (Silicon Guild, 2018). This case study is from a summary of an article by Patty for the Jan-Feb 2014 issue of the Harvard Business Review.

The published summary of that article is as follows.

～

When Netflix executives wrote a PowerPoint deck about the organisation's talent management strategies, the document went viral—it's been viewed more than 5 million times on the web. Now one of those executives, the company's long-time chief talent officer, goes beyond the bullet points to paint a detailed picture of how Netflix attracts, retains, and manages stellar employees. The firm draws on five key tenets:

Hire, reward, and tolerate only fully formed adults. Ask workers to rely on logic and common sense instead of formal policies, whether the issue is communication, time off, or expenses.

Tell the truth about performance. Scrap formal reviews in favour of informal conversations. Offer generous severance rather than holding on to workers whose skills no longer fit your needs.

Managers must build great teams. This is their most important task. Don't rate them on whether they are good mentors or fill out paperwork on time.

Leaders own the job of creating the company culture. You've got to actually model and encourage the behaviour you talk up.

Talent managers should think like businesspeople and innovators first, and like HR people last. Forget throwing parties and handing out T-shirts; make sure every employee understands what the company needs most and exactly what's meant by "high performance."

~

The critical point I want to draw your attention to is the statement following '*Leaders own the job of creating the company culture*.' What Patty is saying is that for Netflix to have created one of the most inspirational company cultures in a modern organisation -

the task fell to 'leaders' to own the job of doing this. They did it primarily by 'modelling the behaviour you talk up'.

The reason for including this case study is to help strengthen the notion that Behaviours build Culture. Remember that you 'get what you measure'? So here is more evidence that if you measure Behaviour (via a KBI) then you get Culture. Period.

6. Surf Live Saving = GREAT

For those who are not familiar with Surf Life Saving Clubs in Australia, let me provide a brief overview. This is a volunteer organisation where members of the general public pay an annual fee to dedicate their spare time, risk their lives, and save the lives of people they have never met, all for zero reward. How unusual! It happens to be the largest such organisation in Australia, where 1.3 million hours of volunteer time help stage over 9,000 rescues a year. Interestingly enough, a rescue is actually seen as a failure as the belief is that real success is advising the public on dangers before they happen, rather than when it is too late. The focus is on achieving fewer rescues through early intervention.

The reason for including this example as a case study is linked to what happens at the annual awards ceremony that most clubs hold at the end of each season. There are no awards for the patrol members who made the most rescues. Nor is there an award or recognition for a patrol member who resuscitated someone after they had drowned in the ocean and been brought back to the beach. But there are awards for people who strive to be the best at their role on the beach, those who embody the spirit of what it means to be a great lifesaver. One of the rewards is the 'encouragement award'. The person who wins this award each year is the person who had the most significant personal battle to achieve what it takes to be a lifesaver. What is actually being rewarded is the behaviours, not the statistics or the outcomes. This organisation is over 100 years old. It has never made a profit in all that time but is united by its culture and powered by its behaviours.

In business, we talk about discretionary effort, where our workforce either works harder or longer than they are contracted to do. When people take pride in their job, the salary becomes a secondary benefit rather than the primary (or only) reason they still turn up every day. How much discretionary effort are we leaving on the table by not inspiring and encouraging our workforce by recognising their positive behaviours and contribution to the culture? I see a role for KBIs in this space.

7. The Canterbury Crusaders = Exceptional

This is an extract from an article written by Kurt Bayer for the Herald newspaper in New Zealand. The reason for including this article is to show what impact can be made on a group of 'average' people when there is a focus on behaviours (via KBIs).

~

Stu Loe was no Flash Harry. Rugged farmer; tough, uncompromising front-rower. A classic country rugby man.

And in the halls of Crusaders' Rugby Park headquarters, Christchurch, on the wall, there he is, front and foremost: Crusader #01. The original. Not a playboy outside back with slick footwork and slicker hair, but Stu Loe. Prop. Man of few words, stranger to hyperbole and bulls***.

But even though Loe retired from rugby last century, and played his last game for the Crusaders 25 years ago – a victorious final at Eden Park that sparked the embers of a sporting dynasty and one of the greatest records in global pro sports – he still carries his old team with him everywhere he goes.

Tucked inside his beaten brown leather wallet is The Brotherhood. Red-and-black core values that Loe helped develop when the Crusaders were struggling, on the pitch, and off it, scrabbling to discover just who they were and what they stood for.

He still carries with him everywhere he goes.

"It's always been in there. I never took it out," the 57-year-old says. "You would turn up to games with your boots, your mouthguard, and your card. It was just part of it."

His thick, calloused fingers skim the printed words that include attitude, honesty, pride, ruthless, relentless, enjoyment, along with some old Japanese wisdom, and, inside, some things that "just need to stay secret".

But that little piece of card, faded and dog-eared, was the foundation on which the Crusaders empire was built. A code of ethics that many others in the brotherhood can rattle off verbatim, and which can reduce some – huge, lumbering men, chockful of brawn and mana – to tears.

And it all started 25 years ago, when the Crusaders could hardly win a game.

The Brotherhood, sometimes referred to as 'The Honesty Card', was the brainchild of up-and-coming coach, and former Canterbury All Blacks first five-eighth Wayne Smith. Smith landed his first major coaching gig at the Canterbury Crusaders (since renamed Crusaders) in 1997. The Lancaster Park-based franchise had struggled badly in the inaugural season of the then Super 12 rugby competition – the dawn of professionalism – finishing dead last, registering just two wins.

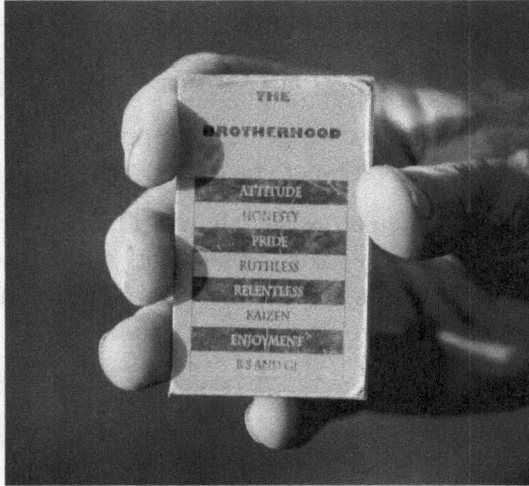

When Smith took the reins, he appointed upcoming rangy loose forward Todd Blackadder as the new captain, replacing the old war horse, All Blacks stalwart and Stu Loe's cousin – Richard Loe. And with sidekick coach Peter Sloane, and Canterbury NPC coach and red-and-black legend Robbie Deans enlisted as team manager, Smith wanted to shake things up.

Smith and Deans, who had played together in Alex 'Grizz' Wyllie's Ranfurly Shield-winning teams of the 80s, thought the players should be united in their goals to be successful and bring together fans from not just across the city of Christchurch, but also the wider Canterbury region, West Coast, Nelson, and Marlborough who also made up the Crusaders franchise catchment area.

Inspiration came from different places. One of Smith's mates was Gilbert Enoka, a pioneering mental skills coach who would forge an international name with the All Blacks, Silver Ferns, Black Caps, and other codes. Smith, who is now known as 'The Professor' for his brilliant, studious, analytical take on the game, got the team to watch a scene from the 1989 film Henry V, directed by Kenneth Branagh.

Based on William Shakespeare's play of the same name, a speech from the historical Battle of Agincourt where King Henry addresses his vastly outnumbered

troops struck a chord for Smith. After the video clip was played to the team, there was silence before the effervescent playmaker Andrew Mehrtens asked if they could watch it again. Loe today finds it difficult to pinpoint just what resonated for them but believes its impact was somehow profound.

"At the time, it was just really relevant," he says. "They [Smith, Deans, Sloane] were ahead of their time in the mental skills approach to the game."

They spent the next week dissecting what they were all about, devising an agreed vision and set of values.

With the Crusaders franchise just two years old, they had no history and little identity. For Smith, it was crucial to find out "what a Crusader man should be", perhaps even more important than coaching.

"We targeted almost a spiritual kinship as our way forward," Smith, the 66-year-old coaching guru told the Herald this week. The players and backroom staff all wrote down what they reckoned it was all about. What they stood for, where they were going, and what would get them there. The thoughts were recorded and distilled to what was eventually 'the honesty card'. Everyone got a copy and had to remember every line.

Smith says they were vision-driven and values based. "We put a huge emphasis on honesty, on living the behaviours we came up with and on keeping each other true to what we were about," he says.

"Because the team was empowered and set their own challenges – with a bit of guidance from coaches! – there was plenty of social capital amongst the players;

sharing of backgrounds, dreams, and aspirations." Smith wanted the players to become true leaders. Some of them have gone on to become top coaches including All Blacks incumbent Scott Robertson, Todd Blackadder, Leon MacDonald, Daryl Gibson, Mark Hammett, Matt Sexton, and Dave Hewett.

But in 1997, when the honesty card was introduced, the Crusaders finished a semi-respectable sixth – a far cry from the wooden spoon the year before – while the Auckland Blues romped to a second successive title.

They had found something though. Auckland was the model. By the time professionalism came to rugby union in 1995, they had been rampant for years. Led by All Blacks legends Sean Fitzpatrick and the Brooke brothers, they owned the Ranfurly Shield from 1985 to 1993 and had built a culture of accountability, along with an enviable depth and competition for places.

The Crusaders' third season started ominously, losing three of their first four games, including a humiliating loss to the Queensland Reds at Ballymore. They started leaning into coach Smith's secret catch cry for the season of 'Kaizen!' – a Japanese term meaning change for the better or continuous improvement.

An "honesty session" at one early training resulted in the team – which had already lost gun halfback Justin Marshall to a season-ending Achilles injury – rallying together and vowing to treat every game as their last in the jersey.

They were early adopters of video analysis. After games, they would dissect why players missed defensive assignments or made glaring errors. It wasn't about piling on criticism but rather working out how to avoid future repeats.

"That all helped build trust in each other, especially in defence," says Loe who played 26 times for the Crusaders between 1996 and 1998. Words are cheap and actions speak louder than words. We could've said lots of things but if you didn't back them up it didn't mean anything."

Aaron 'Oggy' Flynn, the nuggety 90s halfback, stepped in for the hobbled Marshall and remembers the honesty card well. "It was the whole start of things," says Flynn, red-and-black as they come. He ruefully says he lost his card a few years after he retired. "But guys like Stuey [Loe], Toddy, and Marshy and all that, they still all have theirs." They went on a run. There were tough, gritty wins, blowouts, and a legendary away triumph against the Coastal Sharks in Durban where they watched the Henry V battle speech again.

The Crusaders finished the season on a nine-match win streak, culminating in a dramatic final victory over the mighty Auckland Blues at the national fortress, Eden Park.

It sparked a hat-trick run of titles – and a staggering total of 11 over the last 25 years – that has seen the Crusaders become the most successful team in the Super Rugby competition's history.

Todd Blackadder and the Canterbury Crusaders take a tour of Eden Park after the 1998 Super 12 rugby final. Photo / Geoff Dale

On Saturday, they are vying for an unmatched 12th championship. But it all goes back to those early days and the start of the brotherhood. Scott Robertson was a star openside in those late-90s teams and has never forgotten the honesty card and its importance. He famously fashions original themes and goals for every new season, always remembering their origins and those who came before them, guys like Stu Loe. In 2017, during his first season at the helm, Robertson's theme was 'Rumble in the Jungle', based around legendary boxer Muhammad Ali's famous 1974 fight with George Foreman in Zaire. Another year was 'Purple Reign', taking cross-code, cross-Ditch inspiration from the highly successful Melbourne Storm NRL team.

"We've all been coached by lots of different coaches, and you pick out the things that work for you or motivate you and when you get the chance you try and implement them on the next group of players and Scotty Robertson has kept evolving," Loe says.

"I'm not sure just how many themes he's come up with over the years but whatever he does it seems to be working. But it's all about trust and belief and buying into what you're trying to achieve."

The 1998 final was Loe's last appearance for the Crusaders, going on to play one year for the Wellington Hurricanes and, as a Canterbury loan player, over the Southern Alps to help little West Coast qualify top in the NPC third division. When he gave up, he never envisioned the Crusaders' machine becoming the juggernaut of today. "In the early days, there was no real acknowledgement of where this was heading. We didn't know just how special it was going to become. But as the results obviously started rolling in, it did, it really became quite special."

The opening of the new towering Deans Stand at Christchurch's AMI Stadium shortly before the Canterbury earthquakes put the old Lancaster Park out of commission was a turning point in remembering where all the success originated from.

At an official function, ex-players were presented with their franchise number and a piece of rock with a sword thrust into it. Loe, who played loosehead prop in the franchise's first game against the Waikato Chiefs on March 3, 1996, was memorialised as Crusader #01. For the North Canterbury farmer who drove 200km round trips to team trainings in the old amateur days, turning up dusty from a long day's toil, who battled Steve McDowall, Graham Dowd, Olo Brown, and Craig Dowd, who would never express much outward pride, it still clearly means a great deal.

"I guess someone had to be."

~

After this article was written, the Crusaders went on to win their next final, taking their current run of success to 7 titles in a row.

8. Fre'c / C-Two Network = Alternative!

The reason for including this example is to demonstrate how diverse an approach can be to understanding and shaping behaviours within an organisation. Fre'c and the C-Two Network were convenience store chains in Tokyo. They became part of the Tesco group in the early 2000s and were subsequently sold in 2011 when Tesco exited the Japanese market.

The early 2000s was a time when self-checkouts started to become commonplace in Western supermarkets. I was sent to meet with the Japanese management team and share with them the plans, benefits, and impacts that self-checkouts were having in the UK and Central European markets. My expectation was that I would attend a management meeting, deliver my presentation, capture any action points, and plan when (or perhaps 'if') they could adopt these changes into the Japanese business. To be honest, considering how tech-savvy the Japanese market was, I was a bit surprised they were not already there. Regardless, I anticipated an easy presentation.

Unsurprisingly, I was asked to send my presentation ahead of time as pre-read for the management team. No problem.

Upon arriving to give my presentation, I met my interpreter, and we reviewed the presentation materials. Since I couldn't speak Japanese, and although the English proficiency of the Japanese management team was good, it was still more convenient for us to collaborate through an interpreter.

> Just as I was about to inquire if I could start my presentation, my interpreter seemed to anticipate my thoughts and said, "No, please allow the team to discuss first."

Later in the day, as I entered the meeting room to deliver my presentation, I greeted everyone and took a seat at the large round table. I quickly noticed there was no screen to connect my laptop to, and no printed packs to distribute. In fact, each member of the management team had nothing but a single sheet of blank paper in front of them. Just as I was about to inquire if I could start my presentation, my interpreter seemed to anticipate my thoughts and said, "No, please allow the team to discuss first."

One of the leadership team members then said (in Japanese), "Customers are important." What followed was at least a minute of complete silence. I was now on edge, wondering what was happening. Another member of the management team then said, "Time is important." Once again, a prolonged silence ensued, and the faces of the management team displayed intense concentration. This process continued for nearly an hour, with comment after comment being added, each with significant pauses in between for the team to contemplate.

Finally, the allotted time elapsed, and all the management team members stood up, exchanged bows, and quickly left the room. I sat there with my mouth slightly open, appearing a bit dazed. My interpreter sensed my confusion and kindly explained what had transpired.

Since the Japanese management team had read the materials in advance, they easily comprehended the context and purpose of the meeting. Their objective as a group was to discuss what was important to their business and determine whether adopting self-checkouts would benefit them (or more likely - their customers). Without any 'debate' or formal action points documented as 'minutes of the meeting,' the management team's conclusion was clear, unified, and suitable. The answer was a resounding 'no, thanks.'

Thankfully, my interpreter went on to explain more about how the team functioned. Their alignment, cohesiveness, and trust in each other allowed them to engage in discussions like this one with a remarkable depth. Despite their distinct responsibilities, functions, and individual priorities, they were committed to doing what was right for their customers, their market, and their workforce. They didn't need to deliberate extensively; they simply understood. It had

> For this group, the behaviour of 'honouring their customers' was paramount, guiding their decision-making and actions.

taken years for the team to reach this level of alignment, and it was truly impressive.

The reason for sharing this as a case study is to illustrate how behaviours and KBIs can remain pertinent even in the most unconventional ways of operating within an organisation. For this group, the behaviour of 'honouring their customers' was paramount, guiding their decision-making and actions. One of the few metrics they had focused on was 'trust and respect,' which extended to their interactions with one another, their team, and their customers.

HELP!

One example and case study that I am still searching for is how KBIs can support the Agile methodology. To ensure we are on the same page, let me briefly explain what I mean by Agile (as this topic tends to evoke strong emotions among project management professionals!). There is a project methodology known as Waterfall. Essentially, this method involves describing a detailed goal or future state, then allocating resources to step through a process to design, build, test, pilot, and ultimately roll out the product, all within a predetermined time frame and budget. While there may be variations, its core essence is a sequential process with a predetermined end goal or objective. Agile, on the other hand, doesn't have a fixed end state or date. Resources are allocated to enhance the current state through short, focused iterations until the customer is satisfied, resources run out, or other priorities take precedence. Agile initiatives offer numerous benefits, but one common criticism is that they can sometimes become chaotic, consuming resources while making little progress. I believe that aligning the mindset of an Agile team and bringing that alignment through KBIs could enhance the harmony and direction of Agile initiatives. Please let me know if you have a case study that either proves or disproves this hypothesis.

SECTION 10
A Double-Click on Trust

....

Trust is not a behaviour; thus, it should not be a KBI. However, there are behaviours that foster trust. While we touched on the significance of trust earlier, I'd like to revisit and delve a bit deeper into this topic. It holds immense importance.

Some of the most compelling examples of KBI-type initiatives share a common thread: the central goal of cultivating trust. The rationale behind this is quite straightforward. Until a high level of trust is established, any other objectives pursued (even if some transient progress is achieved) are built upon unstable ground that can crumble unexpectedly. This collapse typically occurs at the most inopportune moments, often during periods of intense business stress or significant change.

Here are some points of alignment with others regarding this:

5 Dysfunctions of a Team - Patrick Lencioni

We employed Patrick's pyramid in Section 7 to help us distribute our set of KBIs. Our intention in that section was to target a KBI at the most common catalysts for team dysfunction. By doing so, we can confidently initiate our efforts. We also acknowledged earlier that trust, as the foundation of the pyramid, is likely to emerge as a pivotal concern within your working group.

As mentioned previously, until a critical threshold of trust is reached, engaging in difficult conversations (conflict) and reaching shared understanding and alignment (commitment) becomes challenging. Without these elements, all stakeholders may struggle to collaborate effectively towards a common purpose (accountability) to achieve the desired outcome. The key takeaway here is to recognise that

> Where are you encountering roadblocks in your organisation? Is there extensive conflict and minimal commitment?

"absence of trust = lack of sustainable progress across all the levels built on top of trust."

Where are you encountering roadblocks in your organisation? Is there extensive conflict and minimal commitment? In that case, your focus should be on nurturing Trust. Is there substantial activity but a lack of accountability? Then prioritising Commitment is essential. You might discover that as you address one layer, it exposes issues in the layer below. At some juncture, you will inevitably need to address trust. I'm not proposing that you direct all your KBIs towards a single layer; quite the opposite. The ideal scenario is to have a collection of KBIs spanning all these layers. However, it's acceptable to show a bias, and from my experience, leaning towards trust has consistently yielded positive outcomes. If necessary, you can allocate more attention to one KBI over others, especially if it becomes evident that one layer is weakening. Regardless of the approach, ensure the bedrock of trust remains robust.

Shingo Model

The Shingo model (depicted opposite) lies at the heart of the triumph of the Toyota Production System. Its primary purpose and driving force are to optimise the delivery of 'value,' symbolised in the model as 'Results.' This model illustrates how the interplay among Processes (termed 'Systems' in the Shingo model), Tools, Culture &

Behaviours, and Guiding Principles generates the desired Results. A more detailed model available via Google showcases the connections and roles of the arrows. Notably, Culture (propelled by consistent Behaviours) resides at the core of this model. Devoid of this core, the entire model becomes disjointed. We observe this phenomenon in real life as well. We can all think of instances where a group of people with a strong culture came together and accomplished something remarkable against all odds. Conversely, we can also recall instances where a team possessed all the resources yet fell apart. There's another Shingo model that complements this one, also in the form of a pyramid. The foundation of the Shingo pyramid is termed 'Cultural Enablers.' This aligns with Trust in Patrick's models. Without Respect and Humility, which form the base, the pillars of Improvement, Alignment, and Results cannot stand solidly.

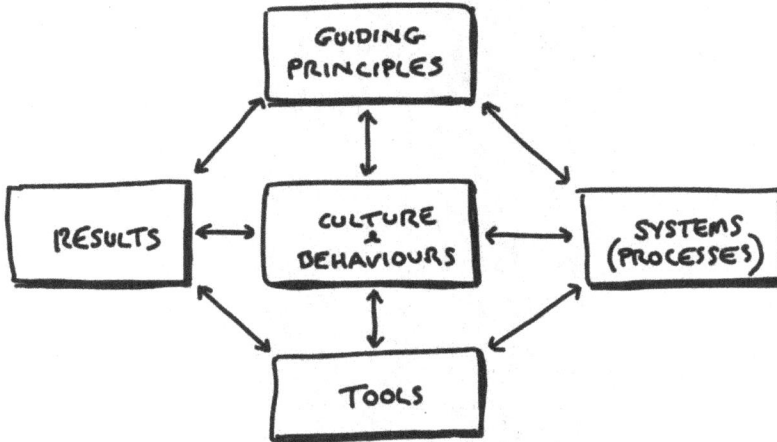

Management in 10 words - Terry Leahy

Under the leadership of Sir Terry Leahy, Tesco became a world super-power of Grocery Retailing. There are, of course, a lot of components that came together to make this happen, and we touched on a few of them in earlier sections. But when you think about the millions of human actions that happened over that timeframe, and you see them boiled down into just 10 words, it is quite amazing. Guess what one of the 10 words is? Yep, another strong vote goes to 'trust' (the 10th word). Please also notice how two other famous Culture Leaders have added their comments to the book. Jack Welch and Alex Ferguson. Jack was the CEO of General Electric when they made some of their most significant gains in some very challenging economic times. Alex was the Manager at Manchester United when they were the dominant force in European football. Both of these leaders are highly respected for building Culture.

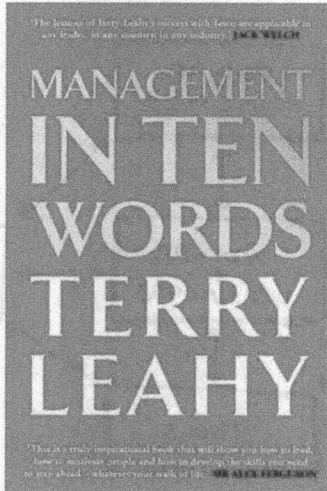

Simon Sinek - Seal Team 6

Please watch the short clip that you can find on YouTube where Simon describes the time that he spent with Navy Seal Team 6.

This team is the best of the absolute best. It is hard to imagine a more demanding situation to work in than this. The stakes are the highest that anyone can play with. The pressure that the team is under must be off-the-charts compared to what business professionals experience on a day-to-day basis. How telling it is then, that in the selection, training, and preparation for these moments of extreme pressure and risk, that the primary logic that is used to determine who makes it into Seal Team 6 is more influenced by Trust than it is by Performance.

You can watch this clip via :

https://www.youtube.com/watch?v=PTo9e3ILmms

NAVY SEAL TEAM 6.

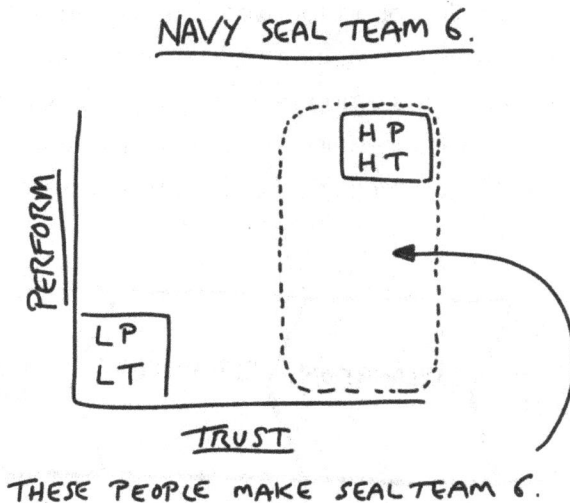

THESE PEOPLE MAKE SEAL TEAM 6.

Simon Sinek - Noah the Barista.

In another clip from Simon, he tells the story of Noah, who works two jobs in two different hotels as a Barista on a coffee cart. He loves one role and barely likes the other one. Again, see the power and impact that trust has on what motivates Noah. Same guy, same role, same everything - just a different level of trust.

You can watch this clip via :

https://www.youtube.com/watch?v=vc4FEIYvkQc

David Orman - How Spies Think.

David is a professor and former director of GCHQ (the British Government Communications Head Quarters). In his book, David explains the methodology and the process that the British Intelligence Service go through to make sense of all the information they pick up from all around the world. A key underlying theme throughout the book is that developing (or at least recognising the level of) trust is paramount in working out what is useful intelligence or distracting noise. This is an incredibly important scenario where the protection of a nation's interests are on the to-do list.

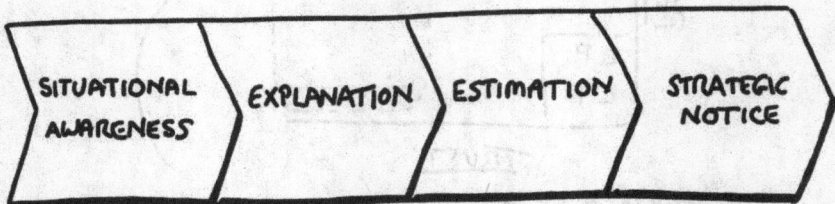

QUOTE: "TRUSTWORTHINESS THEREFORE COMES FROM CONSISTENT, PREDICTABLE, RELIABLE BEHAVIOUR OVER A LONG PERIOD OF TIME, DEMONSTRATING HONESTY COMPETENCE ∧ RELIABILITY."

Again, notice how integral trust is to the overall process. Having trust in the information that comes into the process is just as valuable as having trust in the information as it leaves the process. David specifically calls out that trust is paramount in the initial step of Situational Awareness, and the final step of Strategic Notice. What I also find interesting here is the components that David uses to arrive at 'trustworthiness'. It can be simplified as follows.

Honesty and Competence shown consistently, predictably, and reliably.

David is not alone with his thinking here on what things come together to form up trust. Now, let's have a look at another view of what characteristics go into making up trust. You will see in the follow diagram that two of the key words that David uses are also included. Notice how 'honesty' forms part of the Character branch, while Competence is a branch on its own.

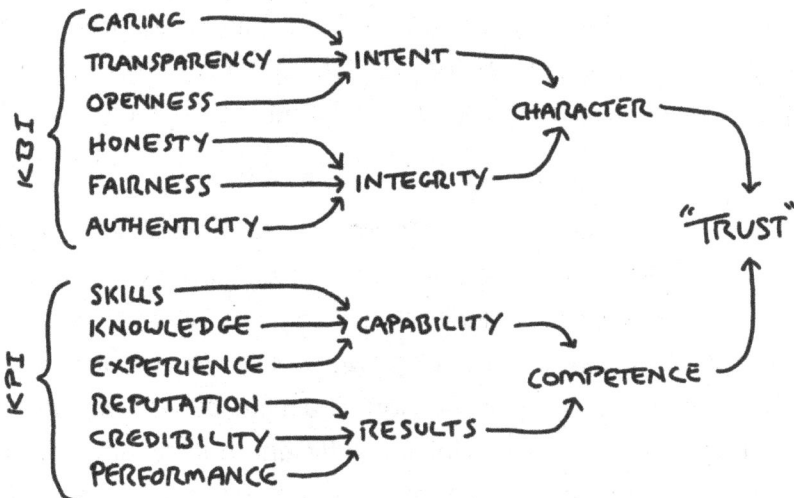

A significant amount of content comes together when we attempt to assess whether we trust someone. We're constantly seeking to identify the boxes we can check off and those we cannot. At times, we try to accomplish this in an instant when encountering new individuals. On other occasions, we allow days, weeks, or even months of interactions to unfold, refining and adjusting our belief in whether we can or should place our trust in that person.

Why is it that we often gauge someone's performance solely based on 'results'? By adopting this approach, we overlook three other pivotal aspects: their actual 'capability,' their 'integrity,' and their 'intent.' It's perhaps no surprise that toxic individuals can ascend through an organisation when we maintain such a limited perspective on their qualities. In section 8, we introduced the Result*Behaviours=STIP formula. This formula introduces balance to the equation above, potentially bolstering and motivating 'exemplary' leaders to persist, while also giving a compelling rationale for 'less effective' leaders to either change or depart.

Observe how the diagram above highlights a branch for KBI (Character) and a branch for KPI (Competence). This serves as another example of how you can have both hands on the steering wheel.

Numerous characteristics contribute to Competence. One can easily envision metrics for them, encompassing skills, experience, and even performance itself. Conversely, character is moulded by qualities that we can correlate with a KBI. When collaborating with the working group in Section 7, aim to convey as much of this insight as possible. Allocate sufficient quality time for the team to determine the optimal KBI options for nurturing and sustaining trust. Perhaps creating one for Intent and Integrity is straightforward, or it might prove more effective to select some at the next level, such as Openness and Authenticity.

Considering the critical role of trust in organisational performance, why would we limit our measurement scope to just half of the contributing factors?

Frances Frei, a Harvard Business School professor, introduces an alternative perspective on the components of trust. As illustrated in the diagram below, Frances outlines the magic triangle of trust: Authenticity, Logic, and Empathy. When any of these aspects wane, trust starts to erode.

> Considering the critical role of trust in organisational performance, why would we limit our measurement scope to just half of the contributing factors?

Once again, you can locate these terms within our dissection of 'Trust.' Authenticity is a direct match, while Logic can align with 'credibility,' and Empathy can correlate with 'Caring.' Two vertices of this triangle lie on the KBI branch of trust, while the third vertex rests on the KPI branch. Hence, Frances suggests that Trust could lean more towards Character than Competency. Reflecting on Simon Sinek's talk on Navy Seal Team 6, this notion certainly holds. Even so, we haven't actively measured this. Why not?

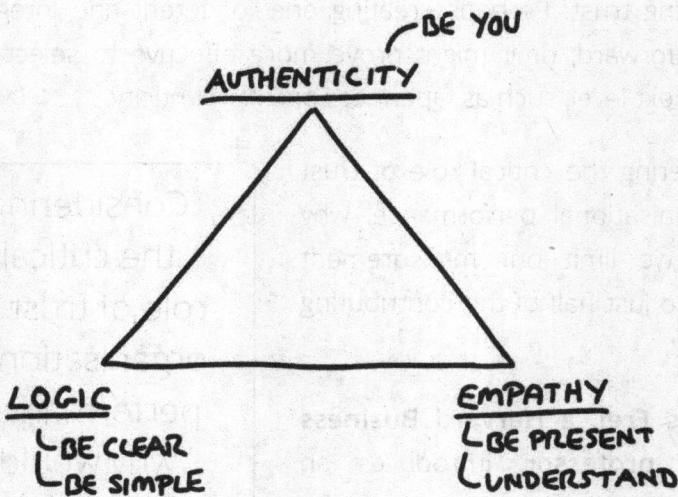

You can watch Frances's clip at

https://www.ted.com/talks/frances_frei_how_to_build_and_rebuild_trust

Frances explains that Empathy is the aspect most commonly missing, yet it's the easiest to work on. This fact holds importance for our KBI work, as human actions related to empathy are easily captured. The two comments underneath, 'being present' and 'understanding', could be captured using a KBI. For 'being present', perhaps all meetings should insist on excluding technology. If participants need to use their laptop or smartphone, they must leave the meeting. A KBI of 'no technology in meetings' would be direct and narrow (but practical), or perhaps 'be present with your teammates' provides a broader context though may not be as straightforward to quantify. For 'understanding', it means asking questions until clarity is reached. How can you support or debate a point without fully understanding the other person's viewpoint? A KBI encouraging 'seeking to understand first' would be an excellent example.

The second most common aspect that tends to falter is Logic. If your logic isn't explained clearly and simply, it can be lost. A KBI promoting clear and simple feedback would support this. An important consideration here is that if your logic is just plain wrong, without trust, no one will bother to tell you. To counter this, a useful approach is to repeatedly ask if your logic makes sense, genuinely listen to feedback, and thank those who challenge it as much as those who agree.

The last aspect, Authenticity, is often lacking to varying degrees. Constantly putting on an act is draining for you and confusing for your team. In times of stress, pressure, or when you revert to your true self, a different version of you emerges, leaving your team wondering about the real story. Being yourself is the only genuine way, but to do so, you need to trust your team. Trust is a circular phenomenon.

Frances's conclusion underscores that behaviours fostering authenticity, empathy, and logical expression are pivotal in building and restoring trust.

A common saying about trust is that you need to 'learn how to trust others.' In the context of KBIs, this approach might not be as constructive. A more effective approach could involve coaching your teams that their responsibility lies in consistently behaving in a manner that enables their teammates to trust them, rather than the other way around. The onus shouldn't be on them to trust individuals who may not prove trustworthy.

IN SUMMARY

There are two motives for revisiting this supremely important topic of trust.

First and foremost, to ensure the success and longevity of this initiative, it's imperative to formulate well-considered key behaviour indicators (KBIs) focused on trust-building. This emphasis will yield the most substantial return on your investment since the link between the behaviours you measure and the outcome of trust-building must remain transparent.

Secondly, considering that the concept of KBIs isn't yet widely prevalent, embracing it as an early adopter entails the added responsibility of swiftly establishing and upholding trust. This is indeed challenging. Rushing or imposing the initiative on the organisation prematurely could jeopardise trust and conflict with KBIs aimed at trust-building. In essence, maintaining consistency in your behaviour throughout this initiative is vital to prevent any semblance of hypocrisy.

SECTION 11
Notes for CEOs

As a CEO, you're already a highly successful individual. It would be widely accepted that you wouldn't have secured your position if you hadn't demonstrated skill, knowledge, experience, and, of course, leadership. The opportunity with KBIs is to now become the best CEO your team has ever worked for, or may ever work for.

While I have no personal experience as a CEO, my role as a CEO coach, a former non-executive board member, and someone who has reported to some excellent as well as not-so-great CEOs allows me to share my perspective on what it takes for CEOs to truly lead and inspire with KBIs, compared to those who merely occupy a seat at the head of the table.

If you're reading this book as a result of KBIs being discussed in your organisation, then please dissect this book comprehensively and become clear and comfortable with the aspects that resonate with you and those that don't. It might be convenient (and less confronting) for me to suggest that you'd only need a minor adjustment to your approach, but that wouldn't be accurate. We're perpetual learners, continuously growing. KBIs present a real shake-up to the system and could potentially challenge your core beliefs. Even if you're nearly the ideal CEO, that only applies to the present. The world keeps evolving, and you must keep up.

The opportunity with KBIs is to revolutionise your relationship with four distinct and vital stakeholder groups.

Group 1: Let's begin with you. Yes, you're a stakeholder in your role. As a CEO, you have internal standards and goals you aspire to achieve, and you're highly motivated to reach them. Chances are you possess a long-standing passion or conviction about who you want to be and why. This initiative provides a genuine chance for you to momentarily hit the pause button, recalibrate, and deeply reflect on what you want to be recognised for and what you aspire to be renowned for moving forward. It's an opportunity for personal realignment. The behaviours that propelled you this far, no matter how effective, might not be the most optimal ones for taking you where you intend to go. How can your team, their teams, and their teams be genuinely inspired and guided by you? Your enduring legacy isn't likely to hinge on a policy, a procedure, or a target (such as a KPI) you've endorsed. It will be a result of your conduct and actions. While KBIs must unquestionably support the organisation's purpose and brand, they also need to align with your authentic aspirations.

> How can your team, their teams, and their teams be genuinely inspired and guided by you?

Group 2: Your superiors. In a substantial organisation, I presume you report to a Board, specifically the Chairman. By spearheading and guiding an initiative on KBIs, you're showcasing profound and influential leadership qualities. This demonstrates to the board that you're proactively managing your most significant asset, the team, and contemplating ways to ensure their future success. In my discussions with fellow board members, this aspect often ranks as the primary concern regarding CEO performance. Skill, knowledge, and experience that qualified you for the CEO role were already widely acknowledged. It's the genuine leadership capacity that remains challenging to assess, even if a CEO has risen through the organisation's ranks. In smaller organisations where there might not be a board above you, there will still be entities, such as the beneficiary organisation of the charity you lead or groups that care about your activities. These individuals will benefit from gaining trust (there's that word again) and confidence that you're committed to the long term and building for the future, not just the upcoming quarter. Your role is pivotal for the organisation's long-term viability.

Group 3: Your team. By wholeheartedly embracing this initiative and transparently prioritising it, you're also supporting numerous other imperatives that probably occupy your agenda. For instance, most CEOs undertake initiatives to enhance areas beyond the "core value chain" of an organisation, like diversity, sustainability, resilience, safety, etc. These aspects are no longer secondary components or optional extras. Unless these elements are actively and openly addressed, your workforce will eventually gravitate towards organisations that do. No one wants to work in an environment where their safety is disregarded, where they need to conform to leadership moulds to advance, or where the planet's future is compromised. With the right set of KBIs, adhered to every day, you'll witness your team aligning with these ideals. This alignment will permeate through their teams. Ultimately, it will loop back to you when a junior team member presents or explains something using the behaviours you're encouraging. What could be more rewarding than that? KBIs, naturally, will also pertain to enhancing the core value chain. Whatever behaviours are required to oil the machinery at the heart of your organisation, this singular initiative will likewise support that.

Group 4: Lastly but absolutely not least, your customers. Sooner or later, word will spread about what type of CEO you are. Your team will express their views about you to customers. Ultimately, your team members return home and converse with their friends and families, who could be customers themselves on their off days. Your duty is to empower team members to highlight the positive attributes you embody, not just lament the paltry pay and the conspicuous absence of company Ferraris. By standing up for them, either directly or indirectly through encouraging a KBI, you're enabling this narrative. Customers make purchases for a myriad of reasons; clearly, price and product constitute the primary motivators. But when these factors are on par, what comes into play next? Arguably, it's trust in the brand, and you possess the opportunity to amplify that trust by steering an organisation recognised for trustworthiness.

One potential pitfall that lies ahead is complacency. The notion that perhaps, when you're with your team privately, you 'don't need to exhibit the behaviours'. The opposite holds true. This is the ideal time to delve deep and wholeheartedly engage when you're behind closed doors with your team. Practice and openly discuss where you observed each of the KBIs being put into practice. This environment provides a secure space for you and your team to cultivate confidence and establish the habit of recognising KBIs in others.

One final reflection before you switch off the lights for the night.

As a CEO, you've likely worked under numerous other CEOs in the past. Which among them do you regard most highly? Who stood out for their achievement of KPIs, and who was renowned for their demeanour? You might expect me to make you choose between the two, but I won't. With KBIs, my suggestion is that you have a pathway to gain recognition for both.

Conclusion

I want to return to the hypothesis from the start of this book.

The hypothesis was as follows:

- Believe that "You get what you measure" is true
- Believe that consistent behaviours define your Culture
- Believe that Culture is critical in achieving your Purpose
- Have behaviours that support your Purpose and Culture
- Observe and measure these behaviours as KBIs
- Lead by example to role model the chosen behaviours
- Capture and report on behaviours using KBIs
- Reward people that role model the chosen behaviours
- Track how these behaviours become dominant
- .... then you win!

Hopefully, by now, by going through this book, you can see a pathway to making this real and it is entirely plausible, and also that you have the confidence to bring it into your organisation.

KBIs are awesome. They are few in number, they cost next to nothing to implement, and their impact is likely to be truly tectonic for the organisation.

KPIs need a haircut. They are suffocating your organisation. Be brave and get rid of as many as you can.

Culture eats Strategy for breakfast. That is a good saying, and very real too. But for many, Culture can be indescribable, too soft, and too mysterious to actually put into words. With KBIs, you can simply and clearly write it down, share it, and explain it. Then you can go further and measure where you are against it.

For an organisation to be successful there are of course many moving parts that need to work in harmony. KBIs alone are unlikely to rescue a failing organisation, or even to turn an average organisation into a fantastic one. There needs to be a critical mass of other good stuff going on. What KBIs will do however, is add something extra to **everything** that is going on, it will amplify the good stuff and give you and your organisation a better chance of winning. It will be your **strategic advantage.**

Over to you.

PS: Please let me know how you get on. I would love to hear how this is brought to life in your organisation. Who knows, maybe the 2nd edition of this book can benefit from some alternative case studies and examples of ways to determine, select, and implement KBIs that shift the needle.

richard.a.perry@icloud.com

Acknowledgements

People

Adam Bentley

Books

Simon Sinek - *Start with Why*

Amy Brann - *Neuroscience for coaches*

James Clear - *Atomic Habits*

Adam Grant - *Think Again*

Patrick Lencioni - *The 5 Dysfunctions of a team*

Charles Duhigg- *The Power of Habit*

Ray Kurzweil - *The Singularity is near*

Yuval Noah Harari - *Sapiens & Homo Deus*

Alexander Osterwalder & Yves Pigneur - *Business Model Generation*

Henrik Fexeus - *The Art of Reading Minds*

Chris Butterworth - *Why Bother*

Terry Leahy - *10 Words*

www.ingramcontent.com/pod-product-compliance
Lightning Source LLC
Chambersburg PA
CBHW011845200326
41597CB00028B/4709